HOW TO
FIND GOD'S
LOVE

BOOKS BY DON NORI SR.

Breaking Generational Curses

Hope of a Nation that Prays

How to Find God's Love

Manifest Presence

Romancing the Divine

Secrets of the Most Holy Place, Volume 1 & 2

Tales of Brokenness

The Angel and the Judgment

The Love Shack

The Prayer God Loves to Answer

You Can Pray in Tongues

AVAILABLE FROM DESTINY IMAGE PUBLISHERS

DON NORI SR

HOW TO
FIND GOD'S
LOVE

DESTINY IMAGE® PUBLISHERS, INC.

P.O. Box 310, Shippensburg, PA 17257-0310

"Speaking to the Purposes of God for this Generation and for the Generations to Come."

This book and all other Destiny Image, Revival Press, MercyPlace, Fresh Bread, Destiny Image Fiction, and Treasure House books are available at Christian bookstores and distributors worldwide.

For a U.S. bookstore nearest you, call 1-800-722-6774.

For more information on foreign distributors, call 717-532-3040.

Or reach us on the Internet: www.destinyimage.com.

Trade Paper ISBN 13: 978-0-7684-3296-1
Hardcover ISBN 13: 978-0-7684-3511-5
Large Print ISBN 13: 978-0-7684-3512-2
Ebook ISBN 13: 978-0-7684-9076-3

For Worldwide Distribution, Printed in the U.S.A.

1 2 3 4 5 6 7 8 9 10 11 / 14 13 12 11 10

DEDICATION

To my dad and mom, Albert and Margaret Nori, who first showed me God's love when I was a child.

To my sons, through whom God continually shows me how simple and free His love really is.

To the one through whom God has proven His consistent, persistent, and ever-growing love to me personally—my precious wife, Cathy.

CONTENTS

PART I

GOD'S LOVE FOR YOU

CHAPTER 1

WHY SEARCH FOR
GOD'S LOVE?

THE SEARCH FOR GOD'S LOVE is the most exciting search anyone can undertake. I know from personal experience. I know because God wants you to have His love even more than you want it! He is all about love. He is all about giving humankind the best He has to offer.

That may seem hard to accept, hard to understand; but God is waiting for you to come to Him so He can lavish His love upon you. Whether you are searching for His love for the first time or you have somehow lost your way, God has His heart and arms open wide—for you. Someone's prayers have been answered—for you. This is your time. This is your opportunity.

And the good news gets even better, for when you seek, you find! When you knock, the door is opened, and when you ask, you get your answer. God is not deaf; He is not far away. He is not too tired or too busy to hear and answer your prayers.

Some people believe that we have to beat a large gong to get God's attention. Others believe that burning incense or lighting candles will make God listen to prayers. But God is not like that at all. He is close to us and hears our every prayer. He knows our deepest needs and our greatest desires. God is so near that He can hear a whispered prayer. He hears every prayer prayed silently, deeply in our hearts. He hears us even in the silence of the night when we lay on our beds. The God of the universe hears our silent prayers as we drift into sleep. That is how close He is and how attentive He is to our needs and desires.

God wants more than anything to answer you and give you deep assurance in your heart that you are loved by Him.

You may have been searching for God's love for many years. On the other hand, you may just be curious as to how someone else feels about God. In either case, this book is in your hands right now because God has answers for you. In fact, you may be reading this because you have prayed to God to show you His love or to show you that He is real.

In my years of knowing God and enjoying fellowship with Him, I have discovered one prayer that God loves to answer. There is one prayer that He will move Heaven and earth to respond to. When someone prays, "Oh God, show me Your love; show me You are real," He will move with great love toward the one who prays that prayer!

There are many folks who spend all their prayers on selfish things like cars, houses, or money. God wants to bless us with all these "earthly" things, but He wants to take care of our inner needs and yearnings first. That's why God loves to answer prayer in a way that results in our knowing Him and enjoying genuine friendship with Him.

People have traveled the world many times over searching for meaning to life, eternal salvation, and love that is real and lasting. Some folks have wealth beyond measure, yet are lonely and empty inside. These people buy for themselves whatever their heart's desire. They go wherever they please. They enjoy party after party. But deep inside, they can be the loneliest and saddest people in the world—what's missing is God's love.

The yearning all people feel in their hearts is for His love, not for things. Those who are wealthy are often disappointed that all their money and all the things they own do not satisfy the yearning in their hearts. "Things" may be fun, but the cry of hearts cannot be satisfied with things—only with God.

Some try to drown their emptiness with alcohol. Others try to avoid the emptiness with drugs. Many search for deep love and lasting friendship in illicit sex, homosexuality, and prostitution. These are all false kinds of love. This kind of earthly love lasts only until a better thrill comes along. They use and abuse both the body and soul, leaving victim after victim scarred and broken. There are no winners in this kind of love. There are no winners because there is not and never will be lasting fulfillment in activities opposed to the harmony in God's order for nature and humankind. God's love fulfills and satisfies the inner desire of every heart.

A NEW DAY

But for you, today is a new day full of hope and promise, because God wants to show His love for you. God wants you to experience His love and enjoy it every day. Today marks the end of your search for His love and the beginning of the answer you have hoped and prayed for as long as you can remember.

God knows all your needs. He cares for you—the real you. It doesn't matter to Him who society or culture says you are. You could be the president of the United States, a movie star, a businessperson, a stay-at-home mom, a student, or a youngster. You could be married, single, or divorced. You may be unemployed. You may be black, white, or brown. God sees your heart and knows everything you need. He sees us all as His children, and He loves, blesses, and cares for all of us equally.

The first thing all people need to acknowledge is that the emptiness deep down inside can only be filled with God's love. The following Bible verse has comforted many people of many centuries: *"So, put first God's kingdom and what is right. Then all the things you need will be given to you. Don't worry about tomorrow, because tomorrow will have its own worries..."* (Matt. 6:33-34). That's a great promise. Let's go for it with all our hearts!

Your Heart Cries Out

The yearnings and achings you feel inside of you to know God are ones that He wants to satisfy. As you read the pages of this book, you will find answers. You will find hope. You will find the reason for living, because you will find God.

I know what I'm talking about. I spent many years with the heartache of loneliness. I tried to satisfy that heartache in many ways. All were dead ends until I discovered the wonder and power of God's incredible love.

I never imagined life could be so different, so hopeful, so rewarding, so full. It happened little by little, step by step. But it happened! It happened for me, and it can happen for you, too!

Let's Pray Together

Dear God, I know that You are real. I know that You are somewhere around me. Please help me find Your love. Please help me to read this book and understand what it is saying deep down in my heart. Please help me not to be afraid. Guide my thoughts as I read, heavenly Father, and show Yourself to me. Thank You for hearing me. Thank You for answering. Amen.

REFLECTIONS

CHAPTER 2

GOD'S GREATEST JOY

YOU MAY BE WONDERING about this chapter title. Do I mean that God has joy? Am I trying to say that He is happy?

Yes, that's exactly what I'm saying. God is a God of joy and peace. He is a God who loves, and who loves to share that love with all humankind. He loves to answer prayers, and He loves it when we enjoy loving Him! God is not the big, mean person we often think He is, or that some were taught He is. He does not stand over you with a big club ready to beat you every time you do something wrong. He does not walk around with a permanent bad attitude about you. He is not scary or unapproachable. God is love! He enjoys His creation. He delights in all that He has made! He doesn't want anyone to perish for eternity, but instead deeply desires all of us to come to know Him personally and intimately. Yes, that means we can be friends with Him. He talks to us and we talk to Him.

His Greatest Joy

God's greatest joy is you! Not many people really think about God from this perspective. Most are concerned only with trying to create and satisfy their own desires and pleasures. Nevertheless, there is joy that God considers His greatest! That "greatest joy" is *you*. God is not too busy keeping the planets in orbit. He is not too busy trying to end wars and famine. He's not too busy counting stars or creating new ones. He doesn't have to find the time to hear your prayer or "squeeze in" your requests between major global events. You are not His hobby. He doesn't only answer you on weekends or His days off. You are not His sideline interest. You are His greatest joy! As a husband enjoys the love of his wife, so God enjoys your love.

He is a personal God whose greatest joy is having us as friends. In the beginning of time, God created Adam and Eve because He wanted someone to talk to. He loved the people He had created and intended them to live with Him in the Garden of Eden forever. When man sinned, that fellowship, or friendship, was broken, although God has always longed to repair it. His love for humankind is powerful and never-ending. God's deepest desire is to have each of us come to Him and experience everything He had planned for us from the very beginning of creation itself. Adam and Eve failed, but we don't have to suffer for their sin. We can experience God's love anyway. Don't be discouraged by what they did. God wants *you* to have His love and joy deep in your heart—forever.

YOUR HOLY DESIRE

It is important that you don't let anyone affect your desire for God. Your desire is nothing for which you should be embarrassed or ashamed. It is a good desire. It is a holy desire. Don't be discouraged if people laugh at you or try to tell you you're crazy for trying to find God's love. Go for it. Follow your heart! God has something special for you—His love.

Many gold-medal winners spend long, lonely years preparing to accomplish and succeed at their chosen goals. While others around them strive for a career, a good income, and secure future, the athlete subjects his body to strain after strain so he or she can be the best, if only for a fleeting moment. You can be the athlete who goes after the "gold" of eternal life. Open your heart and, like the athlete, find the wonderful potential that is yours. But unlike the athletes of this world racing to win, God has already won the ultimate race for you. He is waiting for you at the finish line. Eternity does not begin when you die, it begins the very moment you find His love. He wants you to experience the joy and realize the desire He has for you, right now, in this life.

In a very real sense, just as you are searching for Him, He is searching for you! He wants you to come to Him as much as you want to love and experience Him. Remember, you are His greatest joy. He created you. He loves you. It is delightful to His ears to hear your prayers.

Don't let friends, co-workers, or others squelch that yearning you have for God. It is precious! Even well-meaning clergy can unwittingly cause you to be discouraged in your search for God.

The desire God put in you for Him must not be allowed to go out. Your desire needs to be fanned, not smothered. There is hope for your future. God put you here for a reason. You are His greatest joy. He has dreamed a dream for your life. This dream will fulfill your deepest needs and hopes. He is holding it in His heart, patiently waiting for you to respond to Him. No one else cares for you the way He does. No one can give you fulfillment as He can.

My Desperate Search

Years ago I was in the midst of my own desperate search for the reality of God. I wanted Him more than I wanted anything else. I remember crying night after night for love and a true friend. I often cried out for just one real friend. I wanted someone who would be my friend because he liked me for who I was, not because I was talented, popular, or had some special ability. I had none of those. I didn't want a friend who only wanted to use me. I wanted and needed a Friend.

For the most part, my search was a secret one, since I didn't want to be labeled a religious fanatic or judged as someone with emotional instability. I confided only in one clergyman who served the church where I belonged at the time. He told me that his denomination offered everything of God that there was. There was nothing more.

At first I was very disappointed. Then I got angry. "You mean to tell me," I exploded, "that this is *all* there is to God?!" I couldn't believe that the God who created the entire universe and had made man in His own image and likeness had only lifeless ritual and meaningless traditions to offer me. I couldn't believe that I had spent so many years of my life in a religious system that offered nothing more.

Walking away from that meeting, I was more determined than ever to do what I had to do to find God's perfect love in a personal friendship with Him. I would make any sacrifice and pay any price to find the reality of God that I so desperately desired.

I am not saying that all clergy lack a personal friendship with God. There are millions who have a deep relationship and a solid commitment to Him. They are in the ministry because God called them to do what they are doing. They have a special ability from God to pastor and to care for folks who themselves want to walk with Him.

But I also know that there are some clergy who don't know God. The people they pastor suffer for it. The people faithfully attend church week after week. They hope desperately for a spark of life or reality in God. Week after week they struggle to find God until they find Him on their own or simply give up. Please don't give up. You will find God's love. You will find it before you finish this book!

I strive with all my heart to help people find their destiny in God. I pray with people, counsel them, and encourage them. I often cry with them, feeling their pain as though it were my own. I do all this because I love them as God loves them. I know it pleases God, and I want to please Him—I love Him so much.

WILL GOD EVER GIVE UP ON ME?

You may wonder, *Will God ever forget about me?* I will answer with another question:

*The Always-Present One answers: "Can a woman forget the baby she nurses? No. Does she feel any kindness for the child she gave birth to? Yes. Even if she could forget her children, I would **not** forget you! Look, I have written your name on the palm of My hand. O Jerusalem, I am always thinking about your walls (Isaiah 49:15-16).*

God cannot be anything *but* perfect in His love for you.

Does God really want me to be happy? Does He have good things for me? I will again answer with a question:

Do any of you have a son? What would you do if your son asked you for bread? Would you give him a rock? What if he asked you for a fish? Would you give him a snake? You are evil people, and yet you know how to give good gifts to your children. Surely your heavenly Father knows how to give good things to those people who ask Him (Matthew 7:9-11).

How much more will your Father in Heaven give good things to those who ask? After all, you are His greatest joy!

Let's Pray Together

Dear Lord, thank You for Your love. Although it is hard to understand why I am your greatest joy, I am glad for it. You are my greatest desire. I look forward to knowing You! Help me to receive Your love and Your joy. I am anxious to be part of your family. Amen.

REFLECTIONS

CHAPTER 3

WHY YOU WERE BORN

I SPENT SEVERAL YEARS working in a fast-food restaurant. I also worked in a shoe factory, a printing plant, a supermarket, a meat-packing plant, an amusement park, a newspaper office, a radio station, and as a school teacher. Because I was unfulfilled in my heart, my jobs were difficult to enjoy. I never felt as though I was making a significant and positive contribution to anything in life. I felt as though I could easily die and hardly a person would notice. Worse yet, I also thought that not too many would even care. But those feelings of destitution and gloom were stemming from my frustrations within. I was empty within, and I knew it.

It was easy to take out my tension on those around me. I blamed my parents, my friends, my college professors. I blamed the war in Vietnam and Richard Nixon! But the fault was not in any of these. I blamed everyone but myself.

I did everything except deal with the problem within my own heart. But in reality, it was too scary to deal with the problems inside. That meant I would have to admit that my heart ached. I would have to admit that I was lonely. I'd have to acknowledge to myself that I had few friends and fewer prospective ones. I would have to agree with God that I had failed Him. I would have to admit my sin and my failure to take care of myself and my needs properly. I was a college graduate, working in a dead-end job with no hope of getting a better one.

Yes, to admit my condition would be difficult indeed.

WHY WAS I BORN?

While I was working as a manager in the restaurant, I would often think about my life. I wanted to know why I was born. Each of us were put on this earth with a unique individual destiny to fulfill. I was becoming more and more fearful of never discovering the destiny that was God's plan for me. I thought I was so far from what God's heart was for me that I would never find it. I jokingly look back on those times now, but the fears I had were far from a laughing matter. I would daydream as I walked around the restaurant's kitchen and think, *I can see it all now. My tombstone is sitting tall with this epitaph: HERE LIES DON NORI. HE GAVE THIS TOWN A GOOD PIECE OF CHICKEN.* The thought was horrifying! To think that I could spend my entire life with nothing more to be said of it than that was more than I could handle. I prayed, "Oh God, there's got to be more to You than this. There's got to be more than what the traditional church has to offer. There just *has* to be!"

When God's love came bursting into my heart, I found that there was more, much more. To my great delight, I could feel Him close to me. Deep in my heart, I could hear Him speak to me. There was a peace and an assurance that came over me that I experience even to this day. As time went on and I discovered more about God's love and the dream He dreamt for me; my joy grew. I began to understand that I indeed had a reason to live!

Although all of my problems remained, now I had God. He would help me! There is no greater place of contentment and security than in His arms.

Everything changed at that moment! I rejoiced as well as rested in the knowledge that I was born for a purpose. I knew that there was a destiny for me in God. It didn't matter where I worked or where I lived. God had a plan for me and I was sure of it. Even if I were to stay in that restaurant job the rest of my life, I knew my epitaph would now be vastly different.

I FOUND GOD'S LOVE!

I had found God's love. The whole world looked entirely different than it did before. The job was different.

Even how I looked at myself was different. I had *found* God's love. I realized I had worth. I had value, really. After all, if the God of all creation took a personal interest in me and if He had a personal love for me, how could I keep thinking the same old depressing thoughts? How could I believe the same old lies? How could I feel so worthless if God almighty loved me?

It felt so great to be truly free. I thought God would never forgive all that I had done. I had believed the lie that surely I had committed one too many sins to ever be forgiven by God. But after I found God's love, I didn't feel that way any more. God performed a miracle in me. He changed me and made my life worth living. I knew that I was embarking on a whole new journey in life. No wonder the Bible calls it being "born again"! Everything was new, brand-new. The days and weeks that followed began an incredible unfolding of God's plan for my life. It was exciting, but most importantly, it was real.

He has a plan for you as well. You can never be too young or too old or have committed too many sins to find His love and discover His plan for your life. It is absolutely never too early or too late to start your search.

I know a pastor who was called by God to start a church in a small town in New England. The only space available in town for the church meetings was on the third floor of a downtown building. As they walked to church Sunday after Sunday, they passed an elderly man who was basically living on the streets. As they passed him, they would tell him of God's love and of God's plan for him.

One week the old man finally decided to go to the meeting. It was his day! He found God's love in a mighty way. He stood and cried in gratitude to God and the people who had helped him.

Several weeks later he stood up in church with the following testimony: "One month ago I figured my life was about over. I figured some night I'd fall asleep and just not wake up. I didn't think there was anything for me in this old world. But now everything is different. I know God put me here for a reason. I'm going to find that reason and then do it. I have never been happier."

Too many people think that if all their problems would be solved, they would be happy. But it's just not so. Troubles will always be with us to some degree. It's finding God's love and His purpose that makes life worth living and the troubles worth enduring.

SOMETHING WORTHWHILE

God has a plan for your life—this is an exhilarating thought! God has a plan for you. He has a destiny that is yours alone. Wherever you are in life, whatever job you have, whatever your family, economic, or social status, you were born with destiny.

It is not a prideful feeling to want to do something worthwhile. It is not arrogant to feel God has called you to Himself. He wants you to embrace those feelings because they are real. He has put them in your heart so that you will search them out and discover their reality.

So far we have discovered some incredible truths. We have discovered that God is searching for us and calling us to Himself more intensely than we want Him! Furthermore, not only does He love us, He has a plan for us. He put each one of us on this earth with an individual destiny to fulfill. Simply put, God loves us and has dreamed a wonderful dream for our lives!

In the following chapters we are going to get to the nitty-gritty of how you can actually find His love.

Let's Pray Together

Dear Lord, I know millions have been touched by Your love. They experience Your love everyday. If you have a dream for them, I know you have a dream for me, too. I want that dream. I want Your love. I want everything You have for me. I am opening my heart to You. In Jesus' name, amen.

REFLECTIONS

CHAPTER 4

A MATTER OF HEART

BACK IN THE GARDEN OF EDEN, everything was in order. There was harmony in nature. There was harmony between man and nature and harmony between the man and the woman. There were no sicknesses and no diseases. There was no drudgery or despair. The man and woman did not know fear or anxiety. There was no crime, no greed, and no hate. All of God's creation was in harmony with itself because it was in harmony with God.

The Bible tells us that God often came into the Garden to visit Adam and Eve (see Gen. 3:8). They walked and talked together. They enjoyed each others' friendship and company. All was at peace and all was harmonious.

How far we have fallen since the days of Adam! Adam and Eve's sin of disobedience was the opening of man's sinful nature. This sinful nature in all people has put us in the state we are in today. When people choose to follow God, they soon see the return of God's order in their personal life, family, church, community, nation, and the world. Humankind needs to be brought under control. The Bible says that the heart of man is desperately wicked (see Gen. 6:5). God wants to flood man's *heart* with His love because it is his heart that is the issue. Our *hearts* must change if we are to change.

For instance, passing a law that prohibits murder never stopped anyone from murdering. A person cannot be changed from the outside. He cannot be changed by imposing an external law. The *punishment* that the law commands for lawbreakers is the only thing that keeps people from breaking the law. How many times, for instance, have you gone over the speed limit because you saw no police nearby to give you a fine? That is how the law works—we act a certain way or do a certain thing, not necessarily because we want to, but because there is a punishment if we don't. The heart is desperately sinful; therefore change needs to occur within.

REBELLION

During my rebellious teenage years, I grew my hair long. I enjoyed irritating everyone around me. I knew my parents didn't like it, but it was what I wanted to do. One day Dad approached me with the decree that I had to get my hair cut properly. I respected my dad too highly to put up much of a fight, but I was enraged inside. As I went off to the barber shop I mumbled to myself, "You can make it short on the outside, but it's still long on the inside." I got my hair cut, but the rebellion and anger continued to fester within until I personally found God's love. His love changed my heart and melted the anger and rebellion away as I repented deeply of sins against God and my parents.

Lasting change will never occur through rules and regulations. There must be a change in the heart. For instance, maybe you can remember like I can those dreadful weekends when aunts and uncles and cousins would come to visit. Certain cousins, for one reason or another, were not fun to be around. Anticipating the visits, parents dutifully said to their children, "Your cousins Sally and John are coming today and I want you to play with them and I want you to have fun!" Well, everyone played, but nobody had fun, not even the cousins. Without inner change, there can be no lasting change. Imposed laws, forced friendships, or surface responsibilities never work. The heart is desperately wicked, only God's love can change this truth.

An adult bookstore moved into a neighboring town a few years ago. The moral and religious community was enraged. An organization was formed to picket the store until it moved. Over many months, from early morning to nearly midnight, the picketers were out in force. Even in the depths of winter, they never gave up.

I often pleaded with these people to pray for the owner as much as they picketed. I did not want the man to be forced out only to start a shop somewhere else. I wanted his heart changed so he would find another line of work! I knew that as long as his heart was no different, he would simply move his wares to another city. Maybe if he had been befriended and prayed for he could have found God's love.

Finally, one spring afternoon the local newspaper headline declared that the store had closed. The picketers had apparently won—the building would soon be vacated. The interview with the owner, however, revealed something less than a true victory. He had simply purchased ground in a town 50 miles away and built a bigger store! It was just as I had predicted. He was leaving town more bitter and hateful toward "religion" than he had ever been before. Nobody really won. The man's heart was not changed.

INSIDE OUT

Not only does a sinful heart affect individuals, families, and communities, it affects our nation as well. Most of us want to do what we please. As long as we want to do our own thing and are bent on sinful ways, we will continue to deteriorate as a nation. The sinful heart issue can never be dealt with by changing or adding a law. That has never worked. Congress passes hundreds and hundreds of laws every year and there is still very little positive change. In addition to changing the laws, the heart of the nation and of each lawmaker must change as well.

Although the Bible says that "the heart is desperately wicked," God promises in another part of the Bible, *"I will make this new covenant with the family of Israel," says Yahweh. "After those days, I will put My teachings in their minds. And, I will write them upon their hearts. I will be their God, and they will be My people"* (Jer. 31:33).

This is an exciting promise. God wants to change your heart. He wants to do a miraculous change deep inside of you. He says, *"Also, I will teach you to respect Me completely. I will put a new way of thinking inside you. I will take out the stubborn heart—one that is like stone—from your bodies. And, I will give you an obedient heart of flesh"* (Ezek. 36:26). He wants to give you a soft and tender heart so He can write His laws deep inside of you. Change begins to take place from the inside. When change occurs deep in your heart and in your mind, the external, or the outside, things take care of themselves.

God's love for us is so great that He will do anything to see that change takes place. Consider the following example.

An unwed friend of mine began courting a woman for whom he had great affection and felt he wanted to marry. As time went on, his love grew and grew. He loved to talk about her. I heard this woman's name a dozen times an hour as he recounted the virtues of his would-be wife. He soon discovered, however, that her feelings toward him did not exactly match what he felt in his heart. The next several weeks I witnessed an amazing chain of events as he was determined to win her love. From $500 phone bills to $50 roses to countless 600-mile trips to visit her, the campaign continued unabated. His love for her compelled him to do whatever was necessary to win her. He was willing to pay any price and make any sacrifice. They recently celebrated their first wedding anniversary.

In the same way, God's love for us is so intense, so powerful, and so passionate that He was willing to go to any length and pay any price and do whatever was necessary to win our hearts. He knew that if we were left alone we would never come to Him. Just as my friend knew the woman he loved needed to be pursued, God pursues us.

GOD DID WHAT WE COULD NOT

Can a man change his heart on his own? No, he can't. How can a man choose God's way instead of his own way? He can't do that, either. At least, not without help. Man could not change his own heart, so God came to change man's heart for him. God came to the world in His Son, Jesus Christ. For what man could not do on his own, God did through Jesus.

Now let me point out that if you intend to find God's love, you must lay aside all your old ideas about religion and church. Finding God's love does not mean you simply start going to church. It does not mean you must suffer through lifeless traditions and empty rituals.

Finding God's love is actually finding God Himself. Finding God's love is finding a personal friendship with a personal God. Finding His love is finding Him closely and intimately involved with your day-to-day activities and circumstances. Finding God's love is finding healing and forgiveness of sins. It means finding freedom from bitterness and hatred. It's finding God's strength to walk away from sins and habits that have kept you a prisoner for too many years. Finding God's love means finding true reality and true life. Finding God's love is finding Him through Jesus Christ. Jesus is God's answer for the world. As you can see, finding God's love is far more than a prayer, far more than what you do and don't do. It is the fulfillment of your heart's desire for real friendship with God. Nothing else in the world can fill that God-shaped emptiness within.

The World on Its Own

Left to itself, the world finds itself in chaos, confusion, and on the brink of financial, moral, and nuclear disaster. Man's greed, as well as man's inhumanity to man, has wrought pain and suffering at every turn. Loneliness, depression, and suicide are growing at epidemic proportions worldwide. Yet God's love stands ready to set us free from the hurt and pain we have suffered, or are suffering now. Jesus said, *"I have said these things to you, so that you may have peace in Me. You will have trouble in the world, but be strong; I have conquered the world"* (John 16:33).

Finding God's love is not just a free ticket to a far-away Heaven some day. It does not mean finding mediocre answers and lame excuses. His love is real. It is far more than most of humankind has ever imagined. When God's love is found, the relationship that God had with Adam is restored to you. The friendship and joy of fellowship is as dynamic for us as it was for Adam and Eve. God is not interested in just filling up Heaven. There are already more angels there than are humanly possible to count. God does not need His glory displayed in Heaven, for Heaven is already full of His glory.

God has always wanted to establish friendship with people on earth. God wants Heaven to happen right here and now. When the apostles asked Jesus to teach them to pray, He taught them a prayer that is now said by millions of believers every week—and even every day. Jesus taught them what we know as "The Lord's Prayer." The first part of the prayer follows: *"…Our Father who art in heaven, hallowed be Thy name. Thy kingdom come. Thy will be done, on earth as it is in heaven* (Matt. 6:9-10 NASB).

Did you catch that? God wants life to be the same on earth as it is in Heaven. God wants us to live and enjoy life with Him in the same fullness as folks in Heaven already do. But for most people, even believers who have lost their way, life is far from heavenly. Discovering God's love for the first time or returning to His love is the beginning of a whole new way of living.

When we find His love, God becomes our provider. He becomes our strength, our hope, our joy, and our peace. He heals us, sets us free from fear and anxiety. He clears our minds of unclean thoughts and sinful habits. When we find God's love, we find healing for our whole being. This includes healing our body, soul, and spirit.

> *But He certainly took our suffering upon Himself, and He felt our pain for us. Though we saw His plight, we thought that God was punishing Him. But He was wounded for the things that* **we** *did wrong. He was crushed for the sinful things* **we** *did. The punishment, which made us well, was given to* **Him**! *And, we ourselves are healed by means of* **His** *wounds. We all have wandered away like sheep. Each of us has gone our own*

way. But Yahweh has laid upon Him the guilt of us all (Isaiah 53:4-6).

Let's Pray Together

My Father who art in Heaven, hallowed be Your name. Your kingdom come. Your will be done in earth, as it is in Heaven. Give me my daily bread. And forgive me my debts, as I forgive my debtors. And lead me not into temptation, but deliver me from evil: For Yours is the kingdom, and the power, and the glory, forever. Amen.

REFLECTIONS

CHAPTER 5

WHAT DID JESUS REALLY DO FOR YOU?

WHAT DID JESUS REALLY DO for humankind? More specifically, what did He do for us individually? What did He do for me? What did He do for you? What makes Him any different from others who have come with claims of being someone special?

I am not going to get into complicated details in this chapter. It is important, however, to understand who Jesus is and exactly what He did for humankind—for you specifically.

The Bible says that Jesus is the "*Only Begotten of the Father*" (John 3:16). In other words, Jesus is, in truth, the Son of God. He is pure, holy, without sin, and in perfect harmony with His Father.

Man's separation from God could be changed only through a sinless man. Not only would that man have to be sinless, he would also have to be sacrificed as an offering for sin. The blood of this man was to be used to forgive, cleanse the heart and mind, heal the body, and bring humankind into harmony with God the Father. There was only one Man in the universe, throughout all eternity, who would qualify for this task—the Son of God, Jesus Christ.

Even though Jesus was God's only Son, God made Him the sacrifice who would open the door for you and me to find God's love. The Gospel of John puts it like this: *"God loved the people of the world so much that He gave up His one and only Son. Every person who commits himself to Jesus will not be destroyed. Instead, that person will have eternal life"* (John 3:16). Check out God's love in these verses from the Bible:

> *Since we have been made right with God by faith, we have peace with God through our Lord Jesus Christ. And, hope never disappoints us, because God's love has been poured into our hearts through the Holy Spirit who was given to us. While we were still helpless and ungodly, Christ died for us—at exactly the right time. It is rare when someone dies for another person—even for a good person. However, some do dare to die for a good man. But God reassures us of His love*

for us in this way: While we were still sinners, Christ died for us! Since Christ's blood has made us right with God, even more we will be saved from God's punishment through Christ (Romans 5:1,5-9).

Jesus paid for our sins with His life. He was punished so we would not have to die. When they nailed Him to that cross, the blood He shed washed us clean of our sins. His precious sacrifice makes it possible for us to live in perfect harmony with God. It means we can live in and experience perfect union with God because of Jesus Christ. He comes and takes up permanent residence inside our hearts and gives us indescribable peace.

He heals us, body, soul (emotions), and spirit. He commissions us for service, filling us with His Holy Spirit. He puts us on the road to fulfilling our destiny, the dream God has dreamed for us, and gives us the strength to reach it.

Jesus' sacrifice sets us free from satan's lies and attacks. Jesus crushed satan's head when He arose from the dead. *The devil has no power over anyone who belongs to Jesus.* The days of being tormented by satan are over when we come to Jesus in complete repentance and resolve to go God's way. Mental anguish ends. Voices that sap our strength and fill us with fear are silenced. Lies of our past can no longer torment us.

When you give your heart to Jesus, you are freed from your past. You are a brand-new person, all the old stuff passes away and you begin a whole new life. It does not matter what others say about you or think about you. When you find God's love, you belong to Him. You alone are the judge. Others cannot separate you from Him. In fact, check out this awesome passage of the Bible that speaks of those who find God's love. It has helped me often over the years.

> What should we think about all these things? Since God is for us, who can be against us? God did not keep His own Son. Instead, God gave Him up for all of us. Therefore, wouldn't God give us everything? Who could accuse God's chosen people? God is the One who declares people to be righteous! Who will condemn? Christ Jesus is the One who died and was raised from death. And, He is at God's right side, talking to God for us (Romans 8:31-34).

As if that was not exciting enough, the Bible adds the following just in case you might still doubt what He has done for you:

> Who can separate us from Christ's love? Will trouble, pain, persecution, having no food or clothes, danger, or violence separate us? But, in all these things, we are more than conquerors through the One who loved us. I am sure that nothing will be able to separate us from God's love which is found in Christ Jesus, our Lord—none of

these things—death, life, angels, rulers, the present time, the future, powers, heights, or depth! (Romans 8:35,37-39)

There was such power when God raised Jesus from the dead that the devil's power over humankind was forever crushed. If we will respond to God's love, we can experience the same power that raised Jesus Christ from the dead. This is really true. Countless millions experience this resurrection power every single day. You can, too.

...I will always be with you even to the end of time! (Matthew 28:20)

CHAPTER 6

WHAT IS OUR RESPONSE?

PEOPLE NEED TO KNOW where they are headed before they can realize the need to make changes. We must know we are on the wrong road before we can begin to search out the correct one.

On a family vacation years ago, we found ourselves in just such a situation. My wife, Cathy, was convinced I had taken the wrong exit in southern New Jersey. I was convinced I hadn't. With our boys getting very tired and irritable in the back seat and the car getting low on gas, I stubbornly stayed on the road because I was sure it was the right one. An hour later, I had to admit that Cathy was right (as she usually is!). I only stopped to check the map after I realized beyond a doubt that I was wrong. By then we were way off course. But I needed to be convinced I was lost before I could consider being found.

Please do not go any farther on the course than you are now. It will only get worse. Take it from me, I know from personal experience. As soon as you realize there is a better way, take it!

We already know that man's plans are opposed to God's purposes. We can never find God's love and enjoy walking in it as long as we are on our own paths. The Bible says, "*Yahweh says: 'Indeed, your thoughts are not like My thoughts. Your ways are not like My ways. Just as the heavens are higher than the earth, so are My ways higher than your ways. And, My thoughts are higher than your thoughts'*" (Isa. 55:8-9).

Deep down, people know where they are—lost. Our sin has separated us from God and our stubbornness has caused us to go our own way. We have been unwilling to accept God's provision for us through Jesus Christ. But for those who earnestly desire God's love, the plea from God's own heart is clear. "*So, you should search for Yahweh before it is too late. You should call to Him now while He is near. Evil people should quit being evil. Bad persons should stop thinking evil thoughts. They should return to Yahweh, so that He can have mercy on them. They should come back to our God, because He will freely forgive them*" (Isa. 55:6-7).

A holy God cannot fellowship with us while we are in our sinful condition. That's why the blood of Jesus cleanses us from all sins.

Maybe a story would be helpful.

I live with my family in a rural farming community in south central Pennsylvania. When they were young, my five sons really enjoyed the fields and the woods. They enjoyed being boys. It was not unusual for them to acquire a coating of their day's explorations from head to foot. I sometimes wondered how it was humanly possible to get so dirty in just one day's time.

The most exciting time of the day for the whole family was when Daddy pulled into the driveway. Five boys converged on the car from all directions, running as fast as possible in hopes of being first for their "Daddy's home" hug and kiss.

Sometimes the scenario went like this: I jump out of the car wearing a three-piece suit. When five boys attacked from every direction, there was a gentle but final command to stand still. I know they love me. I understand that I am their father and all they want is some affection. I can appreciate that they have not seen me all day. I love them too. But there must be a separation. Either they clean up and change clothes or they cannot crawl up into my lap. I am clean, clothed in clean clothing. They, on the other hand, are a fascinating mosaic of tar, sand, dirt, and several unknown substances. The two cannot mix! We cannot become one. They cannot tangibly experience the depths of my love for them until after they are cleansed—hugs and lots of loving *followed* bath time.

So it is with God. Without the shedding of the blood of Jesus, there is no forgiveness of sins. When we allow Jesus to cleanse us, to wash us clean, to forgive us our sins, we are prepared to experience God's love. It is really that simple.

Before we go on to the next chapter will you pray this prayer with me?

Let's Pray Together

Dear God, You know how much I want to find Your love. Please help me to understand all that I have read so far. Help me to understand Your love and Your justice. Help me to understand what Jesus really did for me. Help me to see how I need to be forgiven and cleansed of my sins. May Your Holy Spirit bring understanding to me, so I can know the true knowledge of my sin and repentance. In Jesus' name, amen.

REFLECTIONS

CHAPTER 7

A NEW BEGINNING

At this point, it is time to *experience* what I have shared with you. Sometimes new information takes a little longer to understand—please take as much time as you need to read and reread each chapter. This chapter explains how you can experience a new beginning in life—a new start with blessings from God. First, let's discuss a few basics about your new life in God's love.

Repentance is a word little used these days, much less experienced. When I repent of something, I do four things.

First, I admit I did something wrong. No one else did it, I did it. It's no one else's fault, it is my fault. I am responsible for what I did, and I must take responsibility.

Second, I confess my wrong to God. I tell Him clearly and completely.

Third, I ask forgiveness for what I have done. I ask in all humility, knowing that God is under no obligation to forgive me.

Fourth, with all resolve, I commit myself to change. I have seriously resolved to change my actions so as not to offend Him again.

Unless I can come to God under His terms, I will not experience His love. I must be cleansed so that I can draw near to Him and begin to experience the full impact of His love.

So I must come to Him as I am. I must come as a sinner who is separated from God. I must come to Him with the full understanding that I am responsible for the sins I have committed against Him. When that kind of willingness is in my heart, I am ready for a change deep within. God's love and salvation is about to work in me.

The Bible says, *"However, if we admit our sins, then God will forgive us. We can trust God; He does what is right. He will cleanse us from every evil thing"* (1 John 1:9).

We must not confuse our own feelings with what God has said. It is also true that we should not confuse the feelings of others with what God has said. Remember that we are harder on ourselves than God is. We and others are less likely to forgive. But God's love is always moved, motivated by and forever under the influence of His overwhelming love for us individually. He forgives us. Period.

There is no human being who has committed too many sins for God to forgive. There is no stain of sin too hard for Him to wash away. His will is for all people to experience His love. Jesus calls out to humanity in its sinful condition when He says, *"...Learn from Me because I am gentle and humble in heart. You will find rest for your lives. The duty I give you is easy. The load I put upon you is not heavy"* (Matt. 11:29-30).

Does your heart yearn for Him as you read this verse? If you are willing to truly repent of your sins, turn your life over to Jesus, and allow Him to have control of it, then you are ready to experience the beginning of His love.

When you pray the following prayer, or one like it in your own words, the Lord Jesus is with you to hear and answer immediately. You will be changed. A supernatural event is about to happen. God is about to cleanse you, forgive you, heal you, and set you free from the things that keep you from truly living an abundant, joyful, and peaceful life. You are about to be born again.

Let's Pray Together

Dear Heavenly Father, I know that I am a sinner. I know that I have gone my own way. I confess that I have offended You and sinned

against You. I am sorry. Please forgive me. Take
away my guilt and fear. I need Your love. I need
Your mercy and forgiveness. Please come into
my heart. Wash me clean by the blood of Your
Son JESUS. Forgive my selfish ways and help
me to serve You every day. I love You, Lord.
Thank You for forgiving me. Thank You for
coming into my heart. Thank You for saving me!
In Jesus' name, amen.

Jesus said, "*If the Son sets you free, you are truly free*"
(John 8:36). You have called upon the Lord Jesus, who has
set you free from sin and torment. Congratulations! The
Lord Jesus heard your prayer and did what you asked Him
to do. Now you belong to Him. Now you have begun to
experience God's love. That love will grow and grow with
each passing day. Your heart will thrill with the growing
knowledge that Jesus loves you and has accepted you into
His family.

Look at what the Bible says about you now:

The God of peace Himself will make you com-
pletely holy. May He keep your spirit, soul, and
body whole without guilt until our Lord Jesus
*Christ comes. And, He **will** come. God is the One*

who calls you. He is faithful (1 Thessalonians 5:23-24).

You have been tempted the same way all people have been tempted, but God is faithful. He will not allow satan to tempt you with more than you can resist. No, when you are being tempted, God will also give you a way to escape, so that you can endure it (1 Corinthians 10:13).

But the Lord is faithful, He will protect you from the evil one (2 Thessalonians 3:3).

If we are not faithful, He is always faithful, because He must remain true to Himself (2 Timothy 2:13).

Before I was born again, before I really found God's love for the first time in my life, I had quite a reputation as a…well…as a real trouble maker. I was rebellious, angry, hateful, and just an all-around bad person. My behavior was an attempt to hide how lonely and frightened I really was. I was a mess. Some are able to hide what a real mess they are, but not me. If I was going to be miserable, then I wanted everyone around me to be miserable, too!

You see, for me, there was never a moment of inner peace. There was only fear, guilt, and torment. I was afraid of the dark and afraid of people. I was afraid of being alone and afraid of dying. I was afraid of many things. But I realized that I was most afraid of God. I ran because I was afraid of Him. How could He love me? Why would He care? I knew what I had done. I was painfully aware of my sin and separation from God. The fear of God separated me even farther from Him. I didn't have a healthy, respectful fear of God; I had the "Wow, am I screwed!" fear. I thought He hated me and would smite me if He could.

But then I read in the Bible, *"For God so loved the world, that He gave His only begotten Son, that whoever believes in Him shall not perish, but have eternal life"* (John 3:16 NASB). It was so hard to believe He included me in that statement. But somehow, I knew it was my chance. I realized that I didn't have to be afraid. God didn't really hate me, as I thought. He loved me! The Bible said so! I prayed to Him. I told Him my sins, asked Him to forgive me. And to my surprise, He did! He really did! There was such joy in my heart! I was finally right with God! It was thrilling to have all my sins forgiven! No more fear! No more running! God loved me! The weight of a million sins was gone. I felt like I could almost fly; I was so light. I just could not keep such good news to myself. I started telling everyone how I had found God's love!

GOOD NEWS SPREADS FAST

Word spread rather quickly around the university about the change in me. Shortly after I gave my heart to

Jesus, a young woman approached me on campus. Rather sheepishly she said, "Welcome to the Kingdom, brother." I was shocked. "What are you talking about?" I asked. She repeated, "Welcome to the Kingdom, brother." In a bit of frustration I responded, "What do you mean, 'Welcome to the Kingdom'? I don't know what you are talking about!" She looked at me, puzzled, and said, "Aren't you Don Nori?"

"Yes," I said.

"Didn't you find God's love and become born again?"

"Oh, I sure did! Jesus is alive in my heart!" I smiled.

"Well then, that means you are going to Heaven. The devil doesn't have power over you any more. You are not going to hell. Jesus will take you to Heaven when you die!"

I was so excited! I was so engrossed over feeling His love and forgiveness of sins in this life that I did not realize Heaven had anything to do with it! What a deal! I had my sins forgiven. I found God's love. I have friendship with Him. I have freedom from fear and torment *and* I'm going to Heaven! The young lady laughed as she understood I had discovered Heaven as well as a new life on earth.

Your *new life with Jesus* in your heart promises the same future. You too are now free from the clutches of hell to live with God forever. As you continue to seek Him and others who have found God's love, you will undoubtedly grow in your love and devotion to the Lord.

Jesus said, "...*If you are thirsty, come to Me and drink! The person who believes in Me will be like the Scripture that says: 'A river of fresh water will flow from his body'*" (John 7:37-38).

REFLECTIONS

PART II

YOU ARE NOT ALONE

INTRODUCTION

You have just begun to experience God's love. Many, many others have God's love just like you do. There are many who live in your area who enjoy a genuine relationship with Jesus and welcome His love. The following two stories are about people who have found God's love. Maybe you can relate to some of the hassles they had and the things they suffered in their quests for God's love.

CHAPTER 8

MARY'S STORY

RIGHT BEFORE MY SIXTEENTH birthday, I left school for the day and went to work. It wasn't much different from any other day. I was standing at the counter helping some people with their merchandise when my younger sister came in. I looked at her and could tell she had been crying. I stepped away from the counter to ask her what was wrong.

She looked at me for a moment, struggling with the words she had to say. "Mom was on her way home, and something happened. She got stuck on the railroad tracks…a train hit her car…Mary, Mom's dead."

When our stepfather could no longer take care of me and my sister, we moved from foster home to foster home, never really staying very long with any one family. The people we stayed with really wanted to help, but at our ages and with the sudden death of our mother, along with the rejection of our only true father image, we both had a few problems. A void had been created in both our lives from the tragedy. To try and fill that void, we turned to drugs to forget the pain, and to sexual relationships to find the love we so desperately needed. When there are two rebellious teens living in your home, as had our foster parents, who come home drunk or stoned, or the cops bring them home, or they don't come home at all, patience only lasts so long.

Finally things worked out so I could get my own apartment. When the school year was over, my sister moved in with me. So there we were: a seventeen-year-old who had just graduated from high school and a fifteen-year-old, let loose in the world to do as we pleased and go our own way.

What more could a young person want?

A lot.

No matter what we did, the void was still there. No matter how many quarts of alcohol we choked down (and a lot of times it came back up), no matter how many joints we smoked, or how much acid we dropped, no matter how many relationships we had, the void was constantly felt. With a "party 'til you die" attitude, we continued to fool ourselves into thinking that everything was fine, and life couldn't be more fun.

Inevitably we got mixed up with the wrong crowd...
or I should say a *worse* crowd. We were both introduced
to shooting cocaine, and suddenly our life's goal was to
get enough money to stay high. We were living in downtown Houston, stealing, dealing, conning whatever and
whoever we could to keep the dope in our veins. Life was
tough. The only thing that mattered was cocaine. Soon,
though, the streets got rough and vice moved in. The place
was loaded with drag queens, pimps, prostitutes, runaways,
drug pushers, and addicts.

Obviously, someone high up in politics got tired of
looking at all of us and decided to clean house. My sister
got busted twice in the raids and once for trying to sell a
joint to a vice cop. I always seemed to be in the right place
at the right time and avoided any kind of police activity.
Luckily for her, they just slapped her on the wrist and let
her go.

CRYING OUT

With all the police action in Houston, my sister
thought the San Francisco strip in California had to be
a better scene. She decided to go there with a van load
of other kids. She asked me if I would go with her, but I
didn't know what to do. At the time I was dating the guy
who had hooked us both on cocaine. He really loved me

and I loved him too, as long as he could continue to supply my habit. I knew if I left town he would come looking for me, and the thought of his catching up to me was a pretty scary one.

So I found myself in my room on my knees crying out to God to help me. I can remember saying a few prayers in my lifetime. When things really got rough I would cry out to God for help, making promises I never seemed to get around to keeping. But I didn't know what to do. I couldn't get away from this guy, and I couldn't let my sister leave alone. I cried to the Lord for some kind of answer.

Well, this time I had done it. I had opened my big mouth and I was going to get help whether I wanted it or not. I know now that my God is a mighty God and listens to prayers from desperate hearts. Within three days I got an answer to my prayers, and God began to change my life and my circumstances in a drastic way.

The guy I had been dating got into a fight and was stabbed to death. It was a pretty shocking scene to witness, but somehow I seemed to pull through it all right. I talked my sister into going back up north where we had lived before. We were sure there was some kind of action going on, and at least we would know some people. So the day after the funeral, we sold all of our furniture to friends and, with a few hundred dollars, we got on a plane and headed back up north.

Shortly after our arrival, we ran into some old friends who offered us a place to live and met some new friends who could supply us with the dope we both needed. The only problem was that no one shot cocaine and we couldn't get any needles. One day my sister got sick and we went to the emergency room. They left us in the room alone for about half an hour, and within ten minutes we had a dozen needles packed away. Our biggest problem was solved.

About a month later I was walking through town, headed to one of the local bars. A guy pulled over and asked me if I needed a ride. I jumped in. He wasn't overly friendly, but cordial, and graciously went out of his way to drop me off at my destination.

A couple of weeks later, I borrowed a friend's car to go to a convenience store for a snack. When I came out, there was this strange guy sitting in my car. I didn't recognize him at first, but it was the same guy who had given me a lift a few weeks earlier. We talked a little bit, and he asked me if I would like to go to a heavy metal concert the next night. I love rock and roll and quickly accepted—no questions asked. My sister loved concerts even more than I did, so she came along with me.

The guy who invited me was in the band, so he had to set up for the performance; he said he would meet us there. He had a friend of his pick us up. We were all decked out in sparkles, spikes, and heels, ready to rock and roll. When we got there, things seemed a little strange. We were the only ones dressed up, and obviously the only ones who had been partying early that day. Well, the music started and it was definitely heavy metal, but the lyrics were not the average lyrics. About five minutes after the band started playing, my sister and I looked at each other and said, "This is Christian music!" Needless to say, we got a little uncomfortable and left the concert early. Unfortunately, I had a date with this guy after the concert.

Then came the inevitable question, "*Mary, what do you think about God?*" *Well, that was it—you're a nice guy, but I like God just where He's at. He minds His business and I mind mine. He helps me out of jams and I show up in church once every five years. I don't need some God changing things around for me. Anyway, what holy God would want me? Thanks but no thanks, I've been through enough, I thought.*

PRAYERS ANSWERED

But what I didn't know was that this guy and this God would be my destiny. I had already asked for help, and here it came. When I found out the true meaning of Christ and how He loves me, what He did for me at Calvary, and what He wanted to do for me now—I hesitated, took a deep breath, and trustfully accepted Him as my Lord and Savior.

From the moment I asked Jesus into my heart, the guilt and burden of the world was lifted from my shoulders. I was released from the addicting power of cocaine and the addicting power of my lifestyle. I was a slave to sin no more. The Lord was my Protector and my Provider. I found the one and only thing to fill the void in my life. I found the one Person who could truly love me! I found God! I found God's love!

My life has really changed. Each day holds promises of a growing love affair with my Lord. I'm now married to the man I found sitting in my car that night. Most of all, I have a God, a Father who loves me and accepts me, who has changed my life and delivered me from the pit of hell. He is my God, my Father, and my Lover.

Not only has He changed and is changing my life, but He has brought other people like me into my life and has given me the opportunity to share God's love and the saving, loving power of Christ.

As I close this letter to you, I have two questions: Do you feel a void in your life? How are you trying to fill it?

The well-known statement, "God is love," is an understatement! He can deliver you from any circumstance and forgive any sin. Just open your mouth and call on His name!

Jesus said, "*Don't let your heart be troubled. You trust in God; trust in Me, too. There are many rooms in My Father's house. I would have told you, if that were not true. I am taking a trip to prepare a place for you. Since I am leaving to prepare a place for you, you can be sure that I will come back and take you with Me, so that you will be where I am"* (John 14:1-3).

REFLECTIONS

CHAPTER 9

Joey's Story

"OKAY, SLOW POKE, it's your turn," said Mrs. Thomas, my fourth grade teacher. I rose to my feet, walked to the huge blackboard at the front of the class, and proceeded to solve a complex mathematical equation. Before I could finish, Mrs. Thomas instructed me to return to my seat, telling me in front of the whole class that I was the slowest thing she had ever seen.

Needless to say, I was crushed, and I longed for the day when I would be free from her derogatory statements. I really wasn't stupid, but I was a little slower than the other kids. Though I was the same age as they were, I was a good bit smaller, and being what was called a "slow grower" made it very hard on me during those crucial years of childhood.

I couldn't help it if I was smaller and a little slower than the other kids in my class. My mom and dad were relatively small people, so how could anyone expect me to be anything but small also? The fact that I was academically running about a year or so behind the other kids my age made it very hard for me to blend in. I tell you, it was rough—always being left out, bullied by bigger boys—those were hard years.

When I was about 11 years of age, my dad secured a paper route for me in his name. To have it in my own name required that I be 12. So as a scrawny 11-year-old boy, I began to deliver newspapers to approximately 120 customers each afternoon. I was making my own money, taking responsibility for an important job, and was beginning to win the respect of several of the kids who used to ridicule me for being small. The inferiority complex that had shackled me began to fall away, and I started feeling good about myself. But this trend was short-lived.

Every afternoon between 3 and 3:30, I could be found sitting on the corner of Lakewood and Tremor folding newspapers in preparation for delivery. On that corner were several other older paperboys, each folding papers for his particular route. As we sat there folding our papers, the filthy jokes would fly. By this time I was 13, I knew every dirty word you could think of; I also learned a great deal about sex, although I had not experienced it firsthand.

One day, one of the boys brought an X-rated magazine to the corner. I can still remember my first lustful gaze as I turned the pages of that magazine. My heart raced and my mind went wild with sexual fantasy. Something diabolical took root in me that day, and it drove me for years to come. An insatiable thirst for pornography consumed me, and lust drove me like a fierce wind does a wildfire on the open plains. The compulsion was incessant and unrelenting, its tentacles wrapped tightly around my soul.

Actually I was controlled by an unclean spirit determined to keep me captive. The sad truth is that I was merely one young man of millions who have become enslaved by the exploitive powers of the American smut industry.

IDENTITY CRISIS

When I was about 13, my parents got divorced. This catastrophic event sent my sister and me into a tailspin, one from which we have never completely recovered. I couldn't understand why the two people I loved and depended on most in life were doing this to me. I began to question who I really was; and since nobody was telling me, I set out to find the answer for myself. An "identity crisis" took place in my life. Within a year of the divorce my sister moved away to try and straighten out her life. I was living with my mom—my dad and my sister were gone, and the stability I had known as a child had vanished. I was easy prey for any demon that wanted me.

At age 14, I began to drink a few beers at parties with older kids and young adults (in their twenties). My sister returned from her time away; she had failed to put her life back together, and was actively involved in the "jet set" party scene in our section of the city. At 14, I was included in that crowd. Before long, a few beers became a couple of six-packs or a fifth of bourbon, and I was well on my way to becoming a teenage alcoholic.

Also at that time in my life, I became fascinated with the unique sounds of the electric guitar. I was hypnotized by its sounds and captivated by its ability to control and swing moods. As I admired and listened almost nonstop to this unique style of music, I knew what I wanted out of life. The stars who played in the most popular bands had it all! Fame, fortune, all the gorgeous women they wanted. Life seemed so together and full of happiness for them. When I saw Jimi Hendrix in concert at the Allen Shepherd Dome in Virginia Beach in '68, that settled it for me. He was it; I wanted what he had. At 15, I visualized myself on stage before thousands of people and I could hear them chanting my name. As I wooed them with my guitar, I could take my pick of any woman I wanted. My name was in lights, and I was on top of the world. So I bought an electric guitar and set out to make my dream a reality.

About this time I moved to the mountains of Kentucky with my dad, his new wife, and family. Dad had hoped that the move would separate me from destructive influences. But my dream moved with me. Hendrix, beer, partying, and the like remained at the center of my life, and the wholesome surroundings of our sparsely populated mountain community had little positive effect on me. I was headed to hell on a freight train.

I began to lift weights when I was 16, with a diligence unmatched by anyone in my high school. In those days a rock star had to be masculine—none of this sissy stuff you see nowadays. I was getting extremely impressive on the guitar, and weightlifting was making my body look good. All of life appeared to be on an upswing for me, and I thought I was finding the fulfillment I longed for. I was dating the best-looking girls in school, driving one of the fastest cars in the county (although it was my dad's), and winning the respect of many through my guitar-playing skills. I had it made—or so I thought.

In 1970 things began to go sour. First, my idol, Jimi Hendrix, died. On the night he died a friend said in a derogatory fashion, "Hendrix flew the coop, didn't he? Ha…ha…ha!" I wanted to bust the guy in the mouth! The coroner's report revealed Hendrix had suffocated on his own vomit while in a wine- and drug-induced stupor. What a way for a guy to go who was supposed to have it all together! I was crushed; but I picked up the pieces and continued my quest for happiness and lasting fulfillment. True happiness and fulfillment eluded me. It seemed that as I was closing in on what I felt for sure would be maximum joy and pleasure, it would take wings and fly away, placing me at square one once again.

Total Despair

Within a year of Hendrix's death, I developed a severe case of rheumatoid arthritis. As this dreaded disease laid siege on my body, my fingers began swelling and twisting, making guitar playing extremely unbearable at times. The fingers that were once able to fly over the frets on the fingerboard of my guitar now found it hard to find the position of a simple chord. As the arthritis attacked my shoulders and elbows, weight-lifting became a nightmare.

Self-pity that was nothing short of gargantuan overtook me, and total despair earmarked my life. I can remember sitting in my car one night and crying on a girlfriend's shoulder. The pain I was experiencing in my elbow was excruciating, but what was worse was the gloom I saw in my future as the arthritis continued to do its devastating work. I was told I'd be in a wheelchair by the time I was 30 years old; I could find no reason to doubt the prediction. I was a helpless mess.

Not long after that sorrowful night, I met Someone named Jesus. I had known about Him all of my life, but I had never personally met Him. For all I knew, He was a fairytale character like Santa Claus or the Easter Bunny. But on that God-planned night in January 1974, I learned firsthand that He is alive. "He pulled away the clouds that hung like curtains on my eyes, and with one touch He rolled away the stone that held my heart."[1] But please

realize, Jesus did not barge into my life, He simply asked to come in.

For some weeks I had been hearing that my sister, Jill, who was still living in the city where we grew up, had been delivered from her drug addictions and was leading the life of a serious Christian. I couldn't understand that; it scared me.

On January 21, 1974, "by chance" I went with my dad to the city where my sister was living. My grandparents also lived in that city, and so I planned on spending a quiet evening visiting them just like I used to do when I was a kid. On the trip into town, Dad informed me that Jill had arranged to take me to a church meeting where her new pastor was going to be preaching. I was horrified. The last place I wanted to go was to church with her. If she would have wanted to take me to a bar, or to a party with some of her friends, I would have gladly gone, but to a meeting to hear preaching? Not on your life!

When we arrived in town, my dad dropped me off at my grandparents' house and he went on to stay the night with his brother and sister-in-law. After I settled in, I sheepishly asked my granddad if he had heard from my sister recently. "Oh yes," he said, "she called this afternoon and said the meeting she was taking you to was cancelled… something about the preacher's flight not coming in today as expected." I breathed a colossal sigh of relief and settled back for a relaxing evening with my grandparents.

At half-past six, the front door opened and in stepped Jill. Under her arm was a big, black Bible, and on her face was a glow I had never seen before. The last time I had seen her she was a downcast, pot-smoking wino, complete with man problems and a spaced-out brain. Could this be the same girl? I was sure I would find out sooner than later.

After the 11 o'clock news, I said good night and retired to the attic bedroom. The whole evening had been spent in front of the television and not a thing about religion had come up; I was relieved. Just as I was about to reach over from my bed and turn out the light, I heard the patter of little feet ascending the stairway to my bedroom. In walked Jill holding that big, black book—her face glowing. As she entered the room, so did the peace of God, and I was unable to be uptight.

Greatest Source of Joy

The first thing she asked me that night so long ago was, "Joey, if you found the greatest source of joy in the whole world, wouldn't you want to share it with your friends and family? Wouldn't you rush right over to George's house and let him get in on it, too? Wouldn't you want to share it with Mom and Dad?" I nodded my head, and she continued, "Joey, I love you very much, and Jesus loves you."

I began to squirm a little, so she asked me, "If you were to die tonight, where do you think you would go?" My answer didn't seem to surprise her at all; I said, "I'd probably go to hell if there is one." She then asked me what I based that answer on, and I replied, "Because I've been a pretty bad guy; I drink, cuss, and chase women. I'm selfish and self-seeking through and through. If there is a Heaven, I don't deserve to go there, so I guess I'd go to hell."

From my answer, Jill told me the awesome story of the cross of Jesus Christ. She told me that Jesus had been God's offering for the sins of all humankind, and that on the cross He was slain to wipe away my sins. Jesus was crucified, nailed on the cross to die for me and for everybody else. He suffered, shedding His blood, to wash away my sin and make me clean in the sight of God. He took my sin, guilt, and shame, and won God's approval for me. It was something that neither I nor any man could ever hope to do.

Jill asked me if I'd like *to know* that if I died that night in my sleep I would go to Heaven. I answered what I believe any sane person would answer when faced with that question.

"Yes Jill, I'd love to know that."

She told me that if I would turn away from my sin, repent of all I had done, accept Jesus' sacrifice for me as the only possible way I could ever go to Heaven, and receive

Jesus into my heart as my Lord and Savior, then I could be saved. "It's not by being good enough, Joey," she said, "but by accepting what Jesus did for you. When you accept Him into your heart, He gives eternal life to you."

As I sat in quiet meditation on what she had spoken to my heart, she asked me, "Would you like to ask Jesus to come into your heart right now?" I said yes, and gladly bowed my head with her to pray. "Lord Jesus Christ, I come to You as a hell-bound sinner, lifting up to you the fact that You shed Your holy blood on the cross for my sin. Forgive me, Jesus. Come into my heart and into my life by Your Spirit, and make me brand-new. Thank you Jesus, I believe that you do. Amen."

When I finished saying that prayer and lifted my face to smile at Jill, I felt as if a ton of weight had been lifted from my shoulders. A peace I cannot describe with words entered into me and it has never left. I am filled with such an assurance, such a hope, and such a joy unspeakable because of the decision I made that night that I could never return to living life the old way.

I met Jesus that night, and I tell you He's alive. And all that I had done before did not matter anymore. Jesus took all my sins and threw them into a sea of forgetfulness when He hung on that cross. All He was waiting for was the day I would receive Him as my Lord. He feels the same way about you. He longs to get to know you, and for you to get to know Him.

My glorious salvation day was only the beginning of a lot of great things. In His merciful power, God set me free from my addiction to alcohol and my desire for drugs. The bondage to pornography was broken also, and I discovered a desire to live a pure life. I was filled with such a desire to know the ways of my Lord and Savior that I would travel hundreds of miles some weeks in order to sit under the anointed preaching of His Word.

GOD OF HOPE AND HEALING

During the first two years of my Christian life, I began to hear teaching on divine healing. I knew in my heart that it was for me, and that I dare not take it lightly. Time has proven that my life depended on my reaction to the Word of God on healing. Had I rejected it, or even taken it in an indifferent manner, I would probably be a hopeless cripple today. But I received the word *"...with great eagerness, examining the Scriptures daily to see whether these things were so"* (Acts 17:11 NASB). As I searched, I found the Word to be much more than I had ever dreamed possible.

My knowledge concerning divine healing began one night as I was returning home from a softball game. I turned on the little radio in my Datsun pickup and heard a preacher by the name of R.W. Shambach. He was preaching from a couple of verses in Isaiah 53 that said, "Surely

He has born our sicknesses and carried our pains...He was wounded for our transgressions, was bruised for our iniquities, was chastised to obtain peace for us, and with His stripes we are healed!"

As I listened, Shambach explained that when Jesus went to the cross for us, He not only dealt with our sin condition, but our sickness and disease as well. He quoted Psalm 103:3, which states: *"He forgives all of my sins. He heals all of my diseases."* Something went off inside me that night that altered the course of my life. I guess it was faith leaping in my heart. I had believed a lie prior to this night—thinking that I could never be better, that I would only grow worse. The excruciating pain in certain joints and the sight of the swelling, twisting, and gnarling was more than I could stand, so I accepted the prognosis that I was bound for a wheelchair and doomed to a life of misery.

But on the night God arranged for me to hear His servant Shambach, faith came alive, hope was instilled, and a knowledge that would set me free was birthed in my heart. As a ravenous wolf I devoured the Word of God concerning physical healing. Everywhere I looked I saw it plainly. I discovered Hosea 4:6: *"My people are destroyed for lack of knowledge,"* and realized that the ignorance I had previously walked in was my own worst enemy. But no longer was I remaining ignorant. The Lord Jesus who healed people 2,000 years ago was *"the same yesterday, and today, and forever"* (Heb. 13:8). By faith I believed it and my life changed accordingly.

The confession of my mouth began to change, and rather than giving voice to the fears that haunted me and the hopelessness that held me captive, I boldly spoke forth my healing and victory. Jesus began to turn my captivity and I began to experience liberation from arthritis. I came to know, deep within my heart, that healing belongs to me just as surely as forgiveness from sin belongs to me. The blood that Jesus shed at Calvary to wash away my sins was the same blood that He shed at the whipping post to heal me. Regardless of where it was shed on that awesome day, it was Jesus' blood, and every ounce of it worked to set me free from the bonds of satan.

The price Jesus paid was so great, yet humankind continues to spurn what was accomplished as irrelevant and void of the power to be realized on earth. Many believers have put too much of our Christian inheritance off until a future date in Heaven, while all along God's Word declares that He prepares a banquet table for us in the presence of our enemies (see Ps. 23:5). Our enemies are here on the earth, not in Heaven. On that banquet table can be found forgiveness, grace, healing, deliverance from demons, and many other blessings from God. Too often we *"limit the Holy one of Israel"* (Ps. 78:41b NKJV), relegating His blessing back to another era, or putting them off to some future date. But God thunders from the eternal now: *"I am Yahweh who heals you!"* (Exod. 15:26); *"The*

Lord *will provide*" (Gen. 22:14). Jesus *is* the same yesterday, today, and forever.

The Enemy's Attack

Don't for a moment think that gaining such knowledge was all there was to it. When the Word of God takes root in your heart concerning a certain truth, satan will come to contest you. Jesus said he comes immediately to take the Word out of your heart (see Mark 4:15), and his main tools are affliction and persecution. He will slam every contradictory symptom or circumstance that he can right in your face. They will scream out, "The Word's not true! The Word's not true!" But stand your ground, refusing to be moved off your conviction that the Word of God *is* true. Scripture says that *"We live by believing, not by seeing"* (2 Cor. 5:7), showing us the way to victory over what we see with our eyes or feel with the touch. This spiritual principle is seen throughout the Word of God; and if we live by it in every realm of life, we will be pleasing to the Lord (see Heb. 11:6).

And so the enemy attacked; his warfare against me intensifying with each passing day. I remember walking the floor many a night, confessing that the Word of God was true and that by Jesus' stripes I was healed. At times the warfare was so great that I was tempted to despair of life itself, but Jesus was praying that my faith would fail not.

WHEN JESUS PRAYS

When Jesus is praying for you—and according to Romans 8:34, He is—you'll win the fight of faith if you'll *"hold tightly to the hope we said we believed in"* (Heb. 10:23). In time, I began to experience release from the onslaught of arthritis; and as Bible verses on healing were rooted deeply in my heart, all fear and hopelessness left me. I had been told I would be confined to a wheelchair by the time I reached my 30th birthday. I passed the 30th year mark several years ago, and am pleased to report that I never went to that wheelchair. I am as strong today as I've ever been, and I live as a healed and grateful man. *"O give thanks to Yahweh, because He is good. His constant love continues forever"* (Ps. 136:1).

Jesus Christ made all the difference in my life. He loves all of us enough to leave the eternal glories of Heaven and be clothed with a human body. For 33 years He resisted every temptation to sin that is known to man, remaining pure and undefiled in the sight of God His Father. At the right time He submitted to the most horrible kind of death known in that day: death by crucifixion. But that wasn't all. Jesus took upon Himself the sin and sickness of humankind. It all died with Him. He took it to hell, left it there, then His heavenly Father raised Him from the dead!

While Jesus was on the cross He cried, "*My God, My God, why did You abandon Me?*" (Matt. 27:46). For the first and only time in all eternity the special fellowship between Father God and His Son Jesus was broken—when Jesus took our sin upon Himself. It was restored for all eternity when His Father raised Jesus from the dead. On the cross He took it all. He stepped in and took what we deserved—the judgment of God toward our sin. Jesus was judged for us because He carried all our sin. That is how awesome and wonderful His love for us really is!

The Scripture clearly says that a day is coming when this same Jesus will return to earth in great power and majesty to gather His people to Himself and execute judgment on His enemies. His people are those who have received Him; His enemies are those who have not. This selfish world thinks that it is finished with Jesus, but the truth is they haven't begun with Him yet. Jesus Christ is at the end of the road for every man and woman.

My friend, did you pray at the end of Chapter 7?

What Have You Done With Jesus?

What have you done with Jesus? Because He died for you, bearing your sin and shame, because He rose again for you, and because He ascended into Heaven for you, He will save you. You're His choice; now choose Him. A person can breeze through life believing all of this, yet never get around to doing what the Bible says is necessary in order to experience the reality of it. *Knowing* about Jesus is not good enough. *Receiving* Him into your heart is what is required. How do you do that?

1. Repent. That means turn from living life to suit yourself and give it all to Him. Stop going the way you're going, following the wrong crowd—the devil's crowd—and follow Jesus in the way He's going.

2. Believe what the Bible says. It is recorded that God raised Jesus from the dead. The Bible says in Romans 10:9, that we must believe God did this, and we must believe it in our heart. Anything short of this will not do. Also, believe it when you read, *"God has given to us eternal life, and this life is in His Son. He that has the Son has life; but the person who doesn't have the Son of God does not have life"* (1 John 5:11-12). Believe that your only way into life is through God's Son, Jesus Christ.

Too many people believe that God would never accept them. They believe that they have sinned too often or that they have hurt too many people. But I have some incredibly good news. God's love never grows impatient. He never gives up on you! You are never too young, too old, or too bad that He won't bring you to Himself—and you are never so good that you do not need Him.

Pray this prayer, or one like it. Open the door of your heart to Jesus. He loves you. He is waiting for you with His arms and heart wide open.

Lord Jesus Christ, I come to You knowing I'm a sinner. I need Your love, forgiveness, and salvation. I know that You shed Your blood on the cross for my sin. Forgive me, Jesus. I repent, turning from going my own way. I believe God raised You from the dead, and gladly confess You as my Lord. Come into my heart and into my life, by Your Spirit, and make me brand-new. Thank You, Jesus. Amen.

3. Confess Him as Lord. At this point, your new life has begun and Jesus will want to lead you into the all-fulfilling dream He has for you. It amazes me that many of us have spent years and years trying to be good or simply doing things we think will make us

happy. But ultimately we discover that our
way is the wrong way.

As you know by now, you can try everything you
think will make you happy, but it never seems to happen.
Deep inside you are still unhappy, empty, and wandering
through life without advancing toward your God-given
destiny. Give Jesus control of your life. You have searched
for fulfillment in all your own ways; now give Him the
opportunity to prove what He can do for you. Say to Him,
"Lord Jesus, please be my Lord. Take charge of my life, all
of it, and show me what true fulfillment really is." He is
waiting for prayers like that, and He hears every one of
them. He wants nothing more than to give you a life of
fulfillment and meaning. Remember, He has dreamed a
dream for your life. He died and was raised from the dead
so you can fulfill that dream. Please don't waste another
minute.

If the Son sets you free, you are truly free (John
8:36).

Endnote

1. Quote from Keith Green, "Your Love Broke
   Through," *Because of You: Songs of Testimony,*
   Sparrow Records, 1998.

CHAPTER 10

THE FIRST DAY OF THE REST
OF YOUR LIFE

YOU ARE BEGINNING a brand-new life! Praying the prayers in this book is a great beginning to the next exciting chapter in your life. Your past is behind you. Jesus forgives and forgets. Really. Check out these powerful words in the Bible:

> He has taken our sins away from us, as far as the east is from the west. Yahweh has mercy upon those who revere Him, as a father has mercy on his children. He knows how we were made. He remembers that we are dust (Psalm 103:12-14).

> Yahweh says: "Come, let's talk these things over. Your sins are red, but they can be as white as snow. Your sins are bright red, but they can be

white like wool. If you people are willing to obey Me, then you will eat good crops from the land (Isaiah 1:18-19).

Check out these words that Jesus Himself spoke:

God loved the people of the world so much that He gave up His one and only Son. Every person who commits himself to Jesus will not be destroyed. Instead, that person will have eternal life. God did not send His Son into the world to judge it. God sent Jesus so that the people of the world could be saved through Him. The person who commits himself to Jesus is not condemned, but the one who does not commit himself to Jesus has already been condemned, because he has not believed in the name of God's one and only Son (John 3:16-18).

I have come like light into the world, so that every person who believes in Me will not stay in the darkness (John 12:46).

You are tired and have heavy loads. If all of you will come to Me, I will give you rest. Take the job I give you. Learn from Me because I am gentle and humble in heart. You will find rest for your lives. The duty I have for you is easy. The load I put upon you is not heavy (Matthew 11:28-30).

Father, Lord of heaven and earth, I praise You because You have hidden these teachings from the 'wise' and 'intelligent' people, but You show Your teachings to little children. Yes, Father, I praise You, because this is what You really wanted to do (John 11:25-26).

YOUR TOMORROWS BELONG TO JESUS

Your future is in His hands. You no longer have to fear what tomorrow will bring, for God is already there preparing it for you. You have found God's love. Trust in the Lord with all your heart. Don't try to understand Him, but be at peace in the knowledge that He will turn you toward the correct path, whatever that might be. He gives us the desires of our hearts, but He has to get us to where we can see them and understand what it is He has dreamed for us.

I have prayed with hundreds of folks individually who have experienced God's love for the first time. I have watched as the guilt of years of sin and struggle washed away from their hearts and minds. I have seen countless new beginnings, and there is one thing common among them all—they are all different! God has made each one of us uniquely distinctive. The journey you have begun is individually yours. Our Lord will lead you, guide you, help you, bless you, encourage, and most importantly change you into the person you really want to be. It is for this life as well as the next that He came.

You read earlier that when I gave my life to Jesus, I thought it just meant Heaven began the moment I said yes to Him and the dream He dreamed for me. The same is true for you. Heaven is a *now experience* that we should not miss. It is not much fun to simply "hold on" until the end. The Lord has an incredible life planned for you right now. Now that He lives in your heart, He can take you to real fulfillment.

A Prayer for You

Now that you have completed this book and started on your new life with Jesus, allow me to pray for you.

Dear Lord Jesus, thank You for Your love!
Thank you for bringing God's love to the
world, and especially to my friend who has just
completed this book and has begun this new life
with You.

Give strength, hope, faith, and confidence that
You are with everyone who calls on You. Bless

my friend as You have blessed me. Take care, guide, protect, and give wisdom to my friend, as you have done faithfully for me.

Into Your love I commit this prayer and those who have prayed with me. May You bring each dream to pass for each person praying with me in all its completeness. May joy, peace, and fulfillment be with all who love You! In Jesus' precious name, amen.

PART III

READING THE BIBLE

READING THE BIBLE

NOW THERE IS NOTHING more important for you to do than read from the Bible every day. You don't have to read a lot every day, just 15 minutes will help strengthen and build your faith more than you could ever imagine. Of course the more you read, the more the Word will do for you! The Bible is power-packed and overflowing with love, mercy, forgiveness, and hope for your future. The Lord will teach you as you read and give you the confidence you need to believe that *not only* did God dream a dream for you, but He fully intends to bring it to pass in your life time. He will bring it to pass soon enough so you have plenty of time to live it out. God keeps His promises!

To help you get started reading the Bible, here is the Gospel of John, as well as one of my favorite Psalms. I used the Plain English Bible, also called The Great Book, because this translation is easy to read and easy to understand. You will be delighted to see how the Bible comes to life in this translation. In fact, the verses I gave you earlier are from the Plain English Bible, so you already know how easy it is to read and understand.

THE GOSPEL OF JOHN

Jesus

1 ¹In *the* beginning was the Word, and the Word was with God, and the Word was God.² He was with God in the beginning. ³Through him everything was made. Without him nothing which has happened would have happened. ⁴He was the Source of life. That life was light for people. ⁵The light shines in the darkness; the darkness can never put it out!

⁶There was a man named John. He had been sent from God. ⁷This man came to give proof about the light, so that through him, everyone would believe. ⁸John was not the light; *he came* to tell the truth about the light. ⁹The true light was coming into the world. He gives light to every person.

¹⁰He was in the world. Through him the world was made, but the people of the world did not acknowledge him.

¹¹ He came to what was his, but his own people would not accept him.
¹² But he gave the right to become God's children to those who did accept him, to those who believe in his name.
¹³ They were born, not in a human way, from the natural human desire of men, but born of God.
¹⁴ The Word became human and lived among us for a while. We saw his glory, the kind of glory like that of *the* Father's one and only *Son*—full of gracious love and truth.
¹⁵ John was telling the truth about him. John cried out, "This is the man I talked about: 'The one who is coming behind me has been ahead of me,' because he was alive before I was."
¹⁶ We have all received one blessing after another from the fullness of his gracious love. ¹⁷ Though the law was given through Moses, gracious love and truth have come through Jesus Christ. ¹⁸ No one has ever seen God, but Jesus, who is in the arms of the Father, **he** unfolded the story.

IN THE BEGINNING WAS THE WORD, AND
THE WORD WAS WITH GOD, AND THE WORD
WAS GOD (JOHN 1:1).

The Preaching of John

[19] The Jewish leaders from Jerusalem sent some priests and Levites to ask John this question: "Who are you?" This is the proof that John gave:

[20] John did not refuse to answer; he spoke freely. He clearly said, "I am not the Messiah!"

[21] They asked him, "Who are you? Are you Elijah?" John said, "No, I am not Elijah." They asked, "Are you the Prophet?" John answered, "No."

[22] Then they asked him, "Who are you? We must give an answer to the men who sent us here. What do you say about yourself?"

[23] John said, "I am 'a voice shouting in the desert: Prepare the Lord's road,'

Isaiah 40:3

just as Isaiah the prophet said."

[24] (They had been sent from the Pharisee group.)

[25] They asked John, "If you are not the Messiah, Elijah, or the prophet, why are you immersing people?"

[26] John answered them, "Yes, I immerse people in water, but there is another one among you whom you don't know about. [27] He is coming later. I am not worthy to untie his shoelace."

[28] This happened in the town of Bethany (the one across the Jordan River). John was immersing people there.

The Lamb of God

[29] The next day, John saw Jesus coming toward him. John said, "Look, God's Lamb who will take away the world's

sin! [30] This is the one I was talking about: "The man who is coming behind me has been ahead of me, because he was alive before I was.' [31] I didn't know him. Why did I come, immersing people in water? To show him to the people of Israel."

[32] This is the proof that John gave: "I saw the Spirit coming down like a dove from the sky, hovering above him. [33] I didn't know him, but the One who sent me to immerse people in water said to me, 'If you see the Spirit coming down and staying upon someone, **this** is the one who immerses in the Holy Spirit.' [34] I have seen it! I am telling you the truth. **He** is the Son of God!"

Two Men Follow Jesus

[35] Again, on the next day, John stood there with two of his followers.

[36] He looked at Jesus walking by. John said, "Look, God's Lamb!"

[37] When the two followers heard John say this, they followed Jesus.

[38] Jesus turned around and saw them following him. He said to them, "What are you looking for?"

[39] They asked him, "Where do you live, Rabbi? (This word means 'Teacher')." Jesus said to them, "Come and see." So, they went and saw where Jesus was staying. They spent the rest of the day with him. (It was about four o'clock in the afternoon.)

[40] Andrew (Simon Peter's brother) was one of the two men who heard John and followed Jesus. [41] The first thing that Andrew did was to find his own brother, Simon. Andrew

said to him, "We have found the Messiah!" (This word means "Christ.") ⁴² Then Andrew led Peter to Jesus. When Jesus looked at Peter, he said, "You are Simon, John's son. You will be called Cephas." (Translated into Greek, this name means "Peter.")

Nathanael

⁴³ The next day, Jesus decided to leave for the land of Galilee. He found Philip and said to him, "Follow me!" ⁴⁴ Philip was from Bethsaida, the same town where Andrew and Peter lived. ⁴⁵ Philip found Nathanael and told him, "We have found the one of whom Moses wrote in the law. The prophets wrote about him, too! He is Jesus, the son of Joseph, from Nazareth."

⁴⁶ Nathanael said to him, "Is it possible for anything good to come from Nazareth?" Philip said to him, "Come and see *for yourself!*"

⁴⁷ Jesus saw Nathanael coming toward him. Jesus said this about Nathanael: "Look, here is a real man of Israel! There is nothing false about him!"

⁴⁸ Nathanael asked Jesus, "From where do you know me?" Jesus answered him, "Before Philip called you *to come here,* I saw you under that fig tree!"

I AM "A VOICE SHOUTING IN THE DESERT: PREPARE THE LORD'S ROAD," JUST AS ISAIAH THE PROPHET SAID (JOHN 1:23).

[49] And Nathanael answered Jesus, "Rabbi, **you** are the Son of God! **You** are the king of the people of Israel!"

[50] Jesus answered him, "Do you believe because I told you that I saw you under a fig tree? You will see even greater things than this. [51] I am telling you the truth: You will all see heaven open and God's angels coming down and going up from me."

The First Miracle

2 [1] On the third day, in the town of Cana in Galilee, there was a wedding. Jesus' mother was there. [2] Jesus and his followers were invited to the wedding. [3] When the wine was gone, Jesus' mother said to him, "They have no more wine!"

[4] Jesus asked her, "What do you want with me, woman? My time has not yet come."

[5] His mother said to the servants, "Do whatever he tells you."

[6] There were six stone water jars sitting there. (Jewish people used them to make things *ceremonially* pure.) Each water jar could hold about 20 to 30 gallons. [7] Jesus said to them, "Fill the jars with water." They filled the jars to the top. [8] Jesus said to the servants, "Now, pour some of this and take it to the master of ceremonies." They did it. [9] He didn't know where it came from, but the servants who had gotten the water knew. When the master of ceremonies tasted the water which had been changed into wine, he called for the groom. [10] He said to the groom, "Everyone serves the good wine first, and when the people have

had plenty to drink, he serves the cheaper wine. But you have reserved the good wine until now!" ¹¹ This was the first miracle which Jesus performed. It was in the town of Cana in Galilee. Jesus revealed his glory, and his followers believed in him.

¹² After this, Jesus, his mother, his brothers, and his followers went down into the town of Capernaum. They stayed there for a few days.

Jesus Goes to the Temple

¹³ The time for the Jewish Passover Festival was near. Jesus went up to Jerusalem. ¹⁴ He found some men in the temple courtyard. They were selling cattle, sheep, and pigeons. The money-exchangers were also sitting there. ¹⁵ Jesus made a whip from some ropes. He forced all of them to leave the courtyard—even the cattle and the sheep. He turned the money-exchangers' tables over and scattered their coins. ¹⁶ He said to the men who were selling pigeons, "Get those things out of here! Don't turn my Father's house into a place of business." ¹⁷ His followers remembered that this verse was in the Scriptures: "The fire which I feel for Your house burns within me!"

Psalm 69:9

¹⁸ The Jewish leaders asked Jesus this question: "What proof do you give to show us *that you have the authority to do these things?*"

¹⁹ Jesus answered them, "Destroy this temple sanctuary and I will raise it in three days!"

²⁰ Then the Jewish leaders said, "It took 46 years to build

this temple sanctuary—and you would build it again in three days?" [21] (Jesus was talking about his body. [22] After Jesus was raised from death, his followers remembered that he always used to say this. They believed the Scripture and what Jesus had said.)

[23] While Jesus was in Jerusalem during the Passover Festival, many believed in his name. They saw the miracles from God which he was doing. [24-25] Jesus knew what people were like. He didn't need anyone to tell him about men; he always knew what was in man. So, Jesus was not committing himself to them.

Nicodemus

3 [1] There was a man named Nicodemus. He was a Jewish leader, one of the Pharisees. [2] This man came to Jesus at night.

Nicodemus said to him, "Rabbi, we know you are a teacher who has come from God. No one could do these miracles which you are performing, if God were not with him."

[3] Jesus answered him, "I am telling you the truth: If a person is not born again, he cannot see the kingdom of God!"

[4] Nicodemus asked him, "When a man is already old, how can he be reborn? It is not possible for him to go inside his mother's womb the second time and be born!"

[5] Jesus answered, "I am telling you the truth: If a person is not born from water and the Spirit, he cannot enter the kingdom of God! [6] What has been born from men is human. And what has been born from the Spirit is spiritual. [7] Don't be surprised because I said this to you:

'You must be born again.' [8] The wind blows wherever it wishes. You hear the sound of it, but you don't know where it comes from or where it is going. It is the same way with everyone who has been born from the Spirit."

[9] Nicodemus answered Jesus, "How can these things happen?"

[10] Jesus answered him, "Are you a teacher of the people of Israel, and you don't know these things? [11] I am telling you the truth: We are talking about what we know. We are telling the truth about what we have seen. But you are not accepting our truth.

[12] Since I am talking to you about things on earth and you are not believing them, if I were to tell you about heavenly things, how could you believe? [13] I am the only one who ever came down from heaven; no one else has ever gone up to heaven.

[14] Moses lifted up the *brass* snake in the desert *for the people*. In the same way, I must be lifted high, [15] so that everyone who commits himself to me will have eternal life."

[16] God loved the people of the world so much that He gave up His one and only Son. Every person who commits himself to Jesus will not be destroyed. Instead, that person will have eternal life. [17] God did not send His Son into the world to judge it. God sent Jesus, so that the people of the world could be saved through him. [18] The person who commits himself to Jesus is not condemned, but the one who does not commit himself to Jesus has already been condemned, because he has not believed in the name of God's one and only Son.

¹⁹ This is the verdict: Light has come into the world, but people loved darkness more than they loved light because the things which they were doing were evil. ²⁰ Everyone who does evil hates the light. He does not come toward the light. He doesn't want his evil deeds to be exposed.

²¹ But the person who is living the truth comes toward the light. He wants his actions to become clear, because he did them for God.

Jesus Is Greater than John

²² After this, Jesus and his followers went to the land of Judea. He stayed there with them and he was immersing some people. ²³ John was immersing people in the town of Aenon (which is not far from the town of Salim) because there was plenty of water there. People continued coming to be immersed. ²⁴ (John had not yet been thrown into prison.)

²⁵ There was an argument between some of John's followers and a Jewish man about making things pure. ²⁶ They came to John and said to him, "Rabbi, the man you have endorsed, who was with you on the other side of the Jordan River, look, he is immersing people, too. Everyone is coming to him!"

²⁷ John answered, "No one can receive anything if heaven has not given it to him. ²⁸ You yourselves know that I told the truth when I said, 'I am not the Messiah!' I have been sent ahead of him. ²⁹ The groom is the one who will get the bride. The best man is the one who stands by and listens. He is glad when he hears the groom's voice. This

is **my** joy; it is now complete. [30]Jesus must become more important; I will become less important."

Jesus Comes from God

[31]The one who comes from above is greater than all things. The person who comes from the earth belongs to the earth and talks about the earth. The one who comes from heaven is the most important. [32]He tells the truth about what he has seen and heard, but no one accepts his proof.
[33]The person who does accept his proof confirms that God is real. [34]God sent Jesus. Jesus speaks the words of God, because God gave him the Spirit without limit. [35]The Father loves the Son and has put everything in the Son's control. [36]The person who commits himself to the Son has eternal life, but the person who does not obey the Son will not see eternal life. Instead, God's punishment stays on that person.

A Samaritan Woman

4 [1]The Pharisees heard that Jesus was making more followers and immersing more people than John. [2](Jesus was really not the one who performed the immersion; his followers did it.) [3]Jesus left Judea and went back to the land of Galilee.
[4]Jesus needed to go through the land of Samaria. [5]He came to a town in Samaria called Sychar. It was near the property which Jacob had given to Joseph, his son. [6]Jacob's well was there. Jesus was tired because of traveling. So, he sat down for a while at the well. It was about noon.
[7]A Samaritan woman came to get some water. Jesus said

to her, "Please, give me a drink of water." [8] (His followers had gone into town to buy some food.)

[9] The Samaritan woman said to Jesus, "You are a Jewish
man and I am a Samaritan woman. Why are you asking
me for a drink of water?" (Jewish people don't want to
associate with Samaritans.) [10] Jesus answered her, "If you
knew about God's gift and who I really am, **you** would ask
me to give you a drink of living water!"

[11] The woman said to Jesus, "Mister, you don't even have
a bucket and the well is deep. Where are you going to get
this living water? [12] You are not greater than Jacob, our
ancestor, are you? Jacob's flocks and herds, his sons, and
Jacob himself drank from this well. He gave it to us!"

[13] Jesus answered her, "Any person who drinks this water
will become thirsty again, [14] but if anyone drinks the water
which I will give him, he will never be thirsty again. The
water which I give him will become a spring inside him,
welling up to eternal life."

[15] The woman said to Jesus, "Mister, give me some of this
water, so that I won't get thirsty and won't have to come
back here again and again to get water."

[16] Jesus said to her, "Go, call your husband. Then come
back here."

[17] The woman answered him, "I don't have a husband."
Jesus said to her, "So true! [18] You have had five husbands,
and the man you have now is not your husband. You spoke
the truth."

[19] The woman said to him, "Sir, I now understand that you
are a prophet. [20] Our ancestors worshiped on this mountain,

but you *Jews* say that Jerusalem is the place where people must worship."

²¹ Jesus said to her, "Believe me, woman, the time is coming when you won't worship the Father on this mountain or in Jerusalem. ²² You *Samaritans* are worshiping that which you don't understand, but we *Jews* are worshiping what we know. Salvation comes from the Jewish people. ²³ But the time is coming and has now come when the true worshipers will worship the Father in the true, spiritual way. The Father is searching for this kind of people to worship Him. ²⁴ God is spirit. The people who worship God must worship Him in the true way and with the *right* spirit."

²⁵ The woman said to Jesus, "I know that the Messiah (the one called Christ) is coming. When he comes, he will tell us about everything."

²⁶ Jesus said to her, "I am the one!"

²⁷ Just then, Jesus' followers came. They were amazed that Jesus was talking with a woman. However, not one of them asked, "What do you want?" or "Why are you talking with her?"

²⁸ Then the woman left her water bucket and went back into town. This is what she said to people: ²⁹ "Come, see a man who told me everything I've ever done. He must be the Messiah!" ³⁰ So they left town and they were coming to him.

³¹ Meanwhile Jesus' followers were encouraging Jesus *to eat something.* They said, "Rabbi, eat!"

³² But Jesus said to them, "I have some food to eat which you don't know about." ³³ The followers said to one another,

"No one brought Jesus anything to eat, did they?"
[34] Jesus said to them, "I must obey what God wants; He sent me. I must finish His work. **That** is food for me!
[35] "You say, 'Four months more and then the time for harvest comes.' But, listen, I am telling **you** to look up and see the fields. They are ready for harvest now. [36] The person who gathers the harvest receives his pay; he gathers the crops for eternal life. The person who plants and the person who gathers will be happy at the same time. [37] This saying is true: 'One person plants and another person gathers.' [38] I sent you to gather the harvest for which you have not worked. Other men worked hard; you are gaining from their work."
[39] Many Samaritan people in that city believed in Jesus, because of the woman's word. She testified, "He told me everything I ever did!" [40] When the Samaritan men came to Jesus, they were begging him to stay with them. Jesus stayed there for two days. [41] Many more people believed because of Jesus' message. [42] They said to the woman, "We believe, not only because of what you said, but also because we ourselves have heard *Jesus*. We know that he is truly the Savior of the world!"

———————

GOD IS SPIRIT. THE PEOPLE WHO WORSHIP
GOD MUST WORSHIP HIM IN THE TRUE WAY
AND WITH THE RIGHT SPIRIT (JOHN 4:24).

———————

Jesus Heals an Official's Son

⁴³ After two days, Jesus left there to go to the land of Galilee. ⁴⁴ Jesus himself said that this was true: "A prophet is not accepted in his own home town." ⁴⁵ When he came to Galilee, the people of Galilee welcomed him. They had seen all the things he did in Jerusalem at the Passover Festival. (They also went to the feast.)

⁴⁶ Again, Jesus went to the town of Cana in Galilee, where he had changed the water into wine. There was a government official there. He had a son who was sick in the town of Capernaum. ⁴⁷ This man heard that Jesus had arrived in Galilee from the land of Judea. The man came to Jesus and begged him to go down to *Capernaum* and heal his son. (The son was about to die.) ⁴⁸ Jesus said to the man, "You people must see proofs from God and miracles or you will never believe."

⁴⁹ The government official said to Jesus, "Lord, please go down to *Capernaum* before my little boy dies!"

⁵⁰ Jesus answered him, "Go, your son lives." The man believed. He took Jesus at his word and left. ⁵¹ While the man was going down to *Capernaum*, his servants met him. They said, "Your child lives!" ⁵² Then the man began asking them questions about the exact time when the boy got better. They answered, "The fever left him yesterday at one o'clock in the afternoon." ⁵³ The father knew that this was the exact time when Jesus had said, "Your son lives!" The man and his whole family believed.

⁵⁴ This was the second proof that Jesus performed, after he came to Galilee from the land of Judea.

Jesus Heals a Sick Man on the Sabbath Day

5 ¹ Later there was another Jewish festival. Jesus went up to Jerusalem. ² Near the Sheep Gate in Jerusalem there is a pool that is called Bethzatha in the Aramaic language. It has five porches. ³ A crowd of people used to lie around among the porches. Some of them were sick, blind, lame, or crippled. ⁴⁻⁵ One man had been there for 38 years with his sickness. ⁶ When Jesus saw the man lying there, he knew that the man had been there a long time. Jesus asked him, "Do you want to be well?"

⁷ The sick man answered Jesus, "Mister, I don't have anyone to put me into the pool when the water stirs. While I am going, someone else goes ahead of me."

⁸ Jesus said to him, "Get up! Pick up your small bed and walk!"

⁹ Immediately, the man got well. He picked up his bed and began walking around. (This happened on a Sabbath day.)

¹⁰ The Jewish leaders were saying to the man who had been healed, "It is the Sabbath day! It is not right for you to carry your bed."

¹¹ The man answered them, "The one who made me well told me to pick up my bed and walk."

¹² They asked him, "Who is the man who told you to pick up your bed and walk?"

¹³ The man who was healed didn't know who Jesus was,

because Jesus had slipped away in the crowd which was there.

[14] Later Jesus found the man in the temple courtyard. Jesus said to him, "Look, you have been made well.

Stop sinning, so that something worse won't happen to you."

[15] The man went and told the Jewish leaders that Jesus was the one who had made him well. [16] Because of this, the Jewish leaders were persecuting Jesus—he was doing these things on the Sabbath day.

[17] Jesus answered them, "My Father always works and I must work, too."

[18] Because of this, the Jewish leaders were trying even harder to kill Jesus. *They* thought that Jesus was not only breaking *the rules about* the Sabbath day, but he was also claiming that God was his own Father, thus putting himself on the same level with God.

The Father and the Son

[19] So Jesus answered them, "I am telling you the truth: The Son can do nothing on his own. He can only do what he sees the Father doing. Whatever the Father may do, the Son will do the same thing. [20] The Father loves the Son. The Father shows him everything He is doing. The Father will show him even greater deeds than these, so that **you** will be amazed.

[21] Just as the Father raises dead people and makes them live again, in the same way the Son gives life to whom he wishes. [22] The Father does not judge anyone. Instead, He

has given the Son the *right* to judge everything, [23] so that everyone will honor the Son as they honor the Father. The person who does not honor the Son is not honoring the Father who sent the Son.

[24] I am telling you the truth: The person who listens to my teaching and believes in the One who sent me has eternal life. That person is not under condemnation. Instead, he has passed from death over to life. [25] I am telling you the truth: The time is coming—the time has already come—when dead people will hear the voice of the Son of God. And when they hear it, they will live again! [26] The Father has life in Himself. In the same way, He gave life to the Son to have in himself. [27] The Father gave the Son authority to judge, because he is the Son of Man. [28] Don't be surprised at this, because the time is coming when everyone in the graves will hear the voice of the Son of God. [29] They will come out of the graves. Those who lived right will rise to life, but those who did evil things will rise for judgment."

John Told the Truth

[30] "I cannot do anything on my own. I judge on the basis of what I hear. Since I am not seeking my own will, my decision is fair. I am seeking the will of the One who sent me. [31] If I were giving proof about myself, my proof would not be valid. [32] But there is another man who is giving proof about me. I know that the proof he gives for me is valid.

[33] "You *sent some men* to him and he has told the truth. [34] I don't accept proof from human beings. But I am saying

these things, so that you can be saved. [35] John was a light that burns and shines.

You were willing to enjoy his light for a while. [36] But I have more proof than John's—the deeds that I do. The deeds prove that the Father sent me! [37] The One who sent me is the Father; He has given proof about me. You have never heard God's voice. You have never seen His shape. [38] And you don't have His teaching staying in you. You don't believe in the one whom God sent. [39] You are always searching the Scriptures, because you think you will find eternal life in them. But the Scriptures are giving proof about **me**! [40] You don't want to come to me, so that you may have life.

[41] "I don't accept praise from man, [42] but I know you—you don't have love for God in your hearts. [43] I have come with the authority of my Father and you are not accepting me. If someone else comes with his own authority, you will accept him. [44] How can you believe? You accept praise from one another. You are not looking for praise from the only *true* God. [45] Don't think that I will accuse you to your father. Moses is the one you trust. **He** is accusing you! [46] If you believed Moses, you would have believed **me** because he wrote about **me**. If you won't believe in what he wrote, how can you believe in **my** words?"

Jesus Feeds More Than 5,000 People

6 [1] After this, Jesus went back across Lake Galilee (Lake Tiberias).

[2] A large crowd of people was following him, because they saw him perform miracles on sick people. [3] Then Jesus went up on a hill and sat down with his followers. [4] The time for the Jewish Passover Festival was near. [5] Jesus looked up and saw that a large crowd was coming toward him. He said to Philip, "Where can we buy *enough* food to feed so many people?" [6] (Jesus said this to test Philip; Jesus knew what he was going to do.)

[7] Philip answered him, "200 silver coins' worth of food would not be enough—even if each person had only a small amount!"

[8] One of Jesus' followers, Andrew, Simon Peter's brother, said to Jesus, [9] "Here is a little boy who has five small loaves of barley bread and two fish, but how long would that last among so many people?"

[10] Jesus said, "Have the people sit down." (There was a lot of grass in that spot.) There were about 5,000 men. They sat down. [11] Then Jesus took the loaves of bread and gave thanks *to God* for them. He divided them among those who were sitting down. He did the same thing with the fish. They had as much as they wanted. [12] When they were full, Jesus said to his followers, "Gather up the leftovers, so that nothing will be wasted." [13] So, they gathered them up and filled twelve large baskets with the leftover pieces from the five small barley loaves.

[14] The people saw this miracle that Jesus performed. They began saying, "Surely this is the prophet *we were expecting* to come into the world." [15] Jesus knew they were about to

come and take him, so that they could make him a king. So, he left again for the mountains to be alone.

Walking on Water

[16] When it was evening, Jesus' followers went down to the lake.

[17] They climbed into a boat and started across the lake, *heading* for the town of Capernaum. It was already dark and Jesus had not yet come to them. [18] A strong wind was blowing and *the waters of* the lake became rough. [19] Jesus' followers had rowed between 3 and 3½ miles when they saw Jesus. He was walking **on** the lake. He was coming closer to the boat. They were afraid. [20] But Jesus said to them, "Don't be afraid. It is I!" [21] They wanted to take him into the boat, but the boat soon came to the shore where they were heading.

Looking for Jesus

[22] The next day the crowd which had stood on the other side of the lake saw that only one boat was still there. *They knew* that Jesus did not get into that boat with his followers; they had left by themselves. [23] Some more boats from Tiberias came near the place where the people had eaten the bread for which the Lord had given thanks. [24] So, when the crowd realized that Jesus and his followers were not there, they got into some boats and went to Capernaum to look for Jesus.

Everlasting Food

[25] When the people found Jesus on the other side of the lake, they asked him, "Rabbi, when did you come here?"

²⁶ Jesus answered them, "I am telling you the truth: You are looking for me, not because of the miracles but because you ate the food and were filled! ²⁷ Don't work for the kind of food which spoils. Instead, work for the kind of food *which gives you* life forever. I will give you this kind of food. God the Father puts His stamp of approval on me."
²⁸ They asked Jesus, "What should we do, so that we may work God's works?"
²⁹ Jesus answered them, "This is God's work—you must commit yourselves to the one whom God sent!"
³⁰ They said to him, "What miracle will you do, so that we may see it and commit ourselves to you? What will you do? ³¹ Our ancestors ate manna in the desert. It is written: 'He gave them food to eat from heaven.' "
³² Jesus said to them, "I am telling you the truth: Moses did not give you food from heaven. My Father is the One who gives you the true food from heaven. ³³ God's food comes down from heaven and gives life to the world."
³⁴ Then they said to Jesus, "Sir, **always** give us this food!"
³⁵ Jesus said to them, "**I** am the food *which gives* life. The person who comes to me will never be hungry. The one who commits himself to me will **never** be thirsty. ³⁶ I told you, 'Though you have seen me, yet you still do not believe.' ³⁷ All that the Father gives to me comes to **me**. I will never throw out the person who comes to **me**. ³⁸ Why did I come down from heaven? It was not to do what I want to do, but to do the will of the One who sent me. ³⁹ This is the will of the One who sent me: I must not lose anything that God has given to me. I must restore it

to God on the last day. [40] This is what my Father wants: Every person who sees the Son and commits himself to him will have eternal life. I will restore that person on the last day."

[41] The Jewish leaders were complaining about Jesus, because he said, "I am the food which came down from heaven."

[42] They said, "This is Jesus, Joseph's son. We know his father and mother. Why is he now saying, 'I have come down from heaven?' "

[43] Jesus answered them, "Stop complaining among yourselves. [44] No one can come to me, unless the Father who sent me draws him. On the last day I will raise that person *from death*. [45] One of the prophets wrote this: 'All people will be taught by God.'

Isaiah 54:13

Everyone who listens to the Father and learns *from Him* comes to me.

[46] No one has seen the Father. The only one who has seen the Father is the one who was with God. [47] I am telling you the truth: The person who believes has eternal life. [48] I am the food *which gives* life. [49] Our ancestors ate manna in the desert, but they died. [50] There is a *type of* food which comes down from heaven. If someone eats it, he will not die. [51] I am the food which comes down from heaven; *it gives* life. If anyone eats this food, he will live forever. The food which I will give is my flesh. I want the people of the world to live."

[52] The Jewish leaders started arguing strongly with each other, "How can Jesus give us his flesh to eat?"

I AM THE FOOD WHICH GIVES LIFE. THE PERSON WHO COMES TO ME WILL NEVER BE HUNGRY (JOHN 6:35).

[53] Jesus said to them, "I am telling you the truth: If you don't eat my flesh and you don't drink my blood, you do not have life in you! [54] The person who eats my flesh and drinks my blood has eternal life. I will raise him *from death* on the last day. [55] My flesh is real food and my blood is real drink. [56] The person who eats my flesh and drinks my blood stays in me and I stay in him. [57] The living Father sent me. I live because of the Father. In the same way, the person who feeds on me will live because of **me**. [58] This is the food which came down from heaven. The person who eats this food will live forever. This food is not what our ancestors ate and then died."

[59] These are the things which Jesus said while teaching in the synagogue at Capernaum.

Many Quit Following Jesus

[60] Many of Jesus' followers heard these things and said, "This is a hard teaching. Who can obey it?"

[61] Jesus knew that his followers were complaining about this. He asked them, "Does this offend you? [62] Suppose you were to see me going up to where I was before? [63] The Spirit is life-giving; physical things are not worth very much. The words I have spoken to you are Spirit and life,

[64] but some of you don't believe." (From the very beginning Jesus knew who didn't believe and which ones would turn against him.) [65] Jesus said, "This is why I told you that no one could come to me if he were not allowed to come by my Father."

[66] Because of this, many of Jesus' followers turned back. They were not walking with him anymore. [67] Jesus said to the twelve *apostles*, "You don't want to go away, too, do you?"

[68] Simon Peter answered him, "Lord, who else is there to go to? **You** have the words of eternal life! [69] We have believed and know that you are God's holy one." [70] Jesus answered them, "Did I not choose all twelve of you? But one of you is a devil!" [71] Jesus was talking about Judas, the son of Simon Iscariot. Judas, one of the twelve *apostles*, was about to turn against Jesus.

Show Yourself to the World!

7 [1] After this, Jesus was traveling around in the land of Galilee. He didn't want to go to the land of Judea, because the Jewish leaders were trying to kill him. [2] The time for the Jewish Festival of Tents was near. [3] Jesus' brothers said to him, "Get away from here and go to Judea, so that your followers may see the miracles you are doing. [4] If someone wants to be famous, he doesn't hide the things he is doing. Since you are doing these things, show yourself to the world!" [5] (Even Jesus' brothers did not believe in him.)

[6] Then Jesus said to them, "It is not yet the right time for

me. There is always a good time for you. [7] The people of the world cannot hate you.

They hate me because I tell the truth about them—their lives are evil! [8] You should go on up to the feast *in Jerusalem*. I am not going up to this feast just yet. The time is not yet ripe for me." [9] After he said these things, Jesus stayed in the land of Galilee.

Jesus Comes to Jerusalem

[10] After Jesus' brothers went up *to Jerusalem* for the feast, Jesus also went up there, but Jesus did it secretly. [11] The Jewish leaders were looking for him at the festival. They continued to ask, "Where is Jesus?"

[12] Many people in the crowd were arguing about Jesus. Some were saying, "He is a good man." Others were saying, "No, he fools the people!"

[13] But no one was talking about Jesus openly because they were afraid of the Jewish leaders.

[14] The festival was already half over when Jesus came up *to Jerusalem* to the temple. Jesus began to teach the people. [15] The Jewish leaders were amazed. They asked, "How did this man learn so much? He never went to school!"

[16] Then Jesus said to them, "What I am teaching does not belong to me; it comes from the One who sent me. [17] If anyone wants to do what God wants, that person will find out whether my teaching comes from God or if I am speaking on my own. [18] The person who speaks on his own is trying to get glory for himself, but the person who wants glory *to go* to the One who sent him is honest. There is nothing wrong with him.

[19] Moses gave you the law, but not one of you is obeying the law. Why are you trying to kill me?"
[20] The crowd answered, "You are crazy! Who is trying to kill you?"
[21] Jesus answered them, "I did one miracle *on the Sabbath day* and all of you are amazed. [22] Yet you will circumcise a child on the Sabbath day. Moses gave you circumcision! Actually, circumcision did not come from Moses, but from our ancestors. [23] Since a child can receive circumcision on the Sabbath day, so that the law of Moses won't be broken, why are you so angry with me? I made a man completely well on the Sabbath day. [24] Don't judge by the way things look! Judge fairly."

Where Does the Messiah Come From?

[25] Some of the people of Jerusalem were saying, "This is the man whom the Jewish leaders are trying to kill. [26] And look, he speaks in the open and they are saying nothing to him about it. Is it possible that the leaders know he **is** the Messiah? [27] But we know where this man comes from. When the Messiah comes, no one will know where he comes from!"
[28] While Jesus was teaching the people in the temple courtyard, Jesus cried out, "Do you know me? Do you know where I come from? I have not come on my own. However, the One who sent me is true. You don't know Him! [29] But I know Him, because I was with Him. He sent me!"
[30] Then they tried to arrest Jesus. But no one laid a hand on him, because his time had not yet come. [31] Many people

in the crowd believed in Jesus. They said, "When the Messiah comes, will he do more miracles than this man has done?"

Where Will Jesus Go?

[32] The Pharisees heard the crowd arguing these things about Jesus. The most important priests and the Pharisees sent some guards to arrest Jesus. [33] Then Jesus said, "I will be with you a little while longer, but then I must go to the One who sent me. [34] You will look for me, but you won't find me. I will be where you cannot come."

[35] Then the Jewish leaders thought to themselves, "Where is he about to go, so that we cannot find him? He wouldn't go to the Jews who live in the Greek cities, would he? Would he teach non-Jewish people there? Surely not! [36] What is the meaning of what he said: 'You will look for me, but you won't find me' and, 'Where I am, you cannot come'?"

Come, Drink!

[37] On the last and most important day of the festival, Jesus stood and cried out, "If you are thirsty, come to me and drink! [38] The person who believes in me will be like the Scripture which says: 'A river of fresh water will flow from his body.'"

Proverbs 18:4; Isaiah 58:11

[39] (Here Jesus was talking about the Spirit whom the believers were about to receive. The Spirit had not yet *been given*, because Jesus had not yet been *raised* to glory.)

Who Is This Jesus?

⁴⁰ Some of the people in the crowd heard these words. They said, "Surely he is the prophet!"

⁴¹ Other people said, "This man is the Messiah!" Still others said, "The Messiah does not come from the land of Galilee!

⁴² The Scripture said that the coming Messiah would be from David's family and from Bethlehem, the village where David lived." ⁴³ So, the people in the crowd were divided because of Jesus. ⁴⁴ Some of them were wanting to arrest him, but no one laid a hand on him.

Nicodemus Again

⁴⁵ Later the guards came back to the most important priests and Pharisees. They asked the guards, "Why didn't you bring back Jesus?"

⁴⁶ The guards answered, "No man ever spoke like this!"

⁴⁷ The Pharisees answered them, "You haven't been fooled, have you? ⁴⁸ None of the Jewish leaders or the Pharisees have believed in Jesus, have they? ⁴⁹ This crowd is ignorant of the law. They should be condemned!"

⁵⁰ Nicodemus was one of the Pharisees. (*Remember*, he had come to Jesus before.) He said to them, ⁵¹ "Our law does not condemn a man without hearing from him first. We must find out what he is doing."

⁵² They answered Nicodemus, "Are you also from Galilee? Search the *Scriptures* and you will see that no prophet comes from Galilee."

⁵³ Then each one of them went home.

A Woman Caught in Sin

8 [1] Jesus went to Olive Mountain. [2] Early the next morning Jesus went back to the temple courtyard. All the people were coming to him. He sat down and began teaching them. [3] The teachers of the law and the Pharisees brought a woman *to Jesus*. They had caught her committing adultery. They made her stand in the center. [4] They said to Jesus, "Teacher, this woman was caught in the very act of committing adultery. [5] In the law Moses commanded us to stone such people to death. What do **you** say about her?" [6] (They were saying this to test Jesus. They wanted to get something which they could use to accuse him.) Jesus bent down and wrote something on the ground with his finger.

[7] They continued to ask Jesus questions. Jesus stood up and said to them, "The one among you who has not sinned should throw the first stone at her!" [8] Jesus bent down again and continued writing on the ground.

[9] When they heard this, they began to leave one by one from the oldest on down. Jesus was the only one left. The woman was still standing there, too. [10] Jesus stood up and said to her, "Woman, where are they? Is anyone condemning you?"

[11] She answered, "No one, Lord." Jesus said, "I am not condemning you, either. Go, and from now on, don't sin anymore!"

Jesus Is the Light

[12] Jesus spoke to the people again. He said, "I am the light for the people of the world. The person who follows me

will never walk in darkness. Instead, he will have the living light."

[13] Then the Pharisees said to Jesus, "You are testifying on your own behalf; your proof is not valid!"

[14] Jesus answered them, "Even though I am testifying on my own behalf, my proof is *still* valid, because I know where I came from and where I am going. But you don't know where I came from or where I'm going. [15] You judge in a human way; I am not judging anyone *now*. [16] But if I were to judge, my decision would be right, because I am not alone—the Father who sent me is with me, too. [17] And in your law this is written, 'The testimony of two people is valid.'

Deuteronomy 17:6

[18] So, I am testifying on my own behalf and the Father who sent me is testifying for me, too."

[19] The Pharisees asked Jesus, "Where is your father?" Jesus answered, "You don't know me or my Father. If you knew me, you would know my Father."

[20] Jesus spoke these words, while he was teaching in the temple courtyard. He was near the place where the offering boxes were placed. No one arrested Jesus, because his time had not yet come.

I Come From God

[21] Then Jesus said to them again, "I am going away and you will look for me, but you will die in your sins. You cannot come where I am going."

[22] The Jewish leaders asked, "Will he kill himself? He said, 'You cannot come where I am going.' "

[23] Jesus said to them, "You come from below. I come from

above. You come from this world. I do not come from this world. [24] I told you that you would die in your sins. If you don't believe that I am the one, you will die in your sins."

[25] Then they asked, "Who are you?" Jesus answered them, "I am what I have been telling you all along! [26] There are many things I have to judge and to say about you. However, the One who sent me is true. I tell the people in the world only what I have heard from my Father."

[27] They did not understand that Jesus was talking to them about the *heavenly* Father. [28] So Jesus said this to them: "You will know that I am the one when you raise me high. I do nothing on my own. I am only saying the things which the Father teaches me. [29] The One who sent me is with me. He has not left me alone, because I always do what is pleasing to Him." [30] While Jesus was speaking, many people believed in him.

The Truth Frees You

[31] Jesus was talking with the Jews who had believed in him, saying, "If you stay with my teaching, you are truly my followers. [32] You will find out the truth, and the truth will set you free."

[33] They answered him, "We are Abraham's descendants. We have never been slaves. How can you say, 'You will be free'?"

[34] Jesus answered them, "I am telling you the truth: Every person who continues to sin is a slave of sin. [35] A slave does not live in the house forever, but a son will always live there. [36] If the Son sets you free, you are truly free.

[37] I know that you are descendants of Abraham, but you are trying to kill me because you cannot find room in your hearts for my teaching. [38] I talk about the things which I saw while I was with the Father. You do the things which you hear from your father.

[39] They answered Jesus, "Abraham is our father!" Jesus said to them, "If you were Abraham's children, you would be doing the things that Abraham did. [40] Abraham would not have done this, but now you are trying to kill me. I have told you the truth which I heard when I was with God. [41] You are doing the things your father does." They said to Jesus, "The only Father we have is God; we are not illegitimate!"

[42] Jesus said to them, "If God were your Father, you would love me. I am here now and I came from God. I didn't come on my own; God sent me. [43] Why do you not understand what I am saying? You cannot obey my teaching. [44] You come from your father, the Devil. You want to do the sinful things that your father wants. The Devil was a murderer from the very beginning. He does not stand with the truth, because there is no truth in him. When he tells a lie, he is only talking naturally, because he is a liar and the father of lies.

[45] "But I am telling you the truth and that is why you don't believe me.

[46] Can one of you prove that I am guilty of sin? Since I *always* tell the truth, why do you not believe me? [47] The person who comes from God listens to God. This is why you won't listen—you are not from God!"

I Lived Before Abraham Did

⁴⁸ The Jewish leaders answered, "How right we are when we say that you are a Samaritan; you are crazy!"

⁴⁹ Jesus answered, "I am not crazy. I honor my Father, but you don't honor me. ⁵⁰ I'm not looking for glory for myself, but there is One who is looking for *glory for me*; He is the Judge. ⁵¹ I am telling you the truth: If anyone obeys my teaching, he will **never** die!"

⁵² Then the Jewish leaders said to Jesus, "Now we **know** that you are crazy! Abraham and the prophets died. Yet you say, 'If anyone obeys my teaching, he will **never** die.' ⁵³ You are not more important than Abraham, our ancestor, are you? He died. The prophets died, too. Just who do you think you are?"

⁵⁴ Jesus answered, "If I *were trying* to get glory for myself, my glory would be *worth* nothing. The One who is giving me glory is my Father. You are saying, 'He is our God!' ⁵⁵ But you don't know Him. I know Him. If I were to say that I do not know Him, I would be like you—a liar! But I really do know Him and I obey His teaching. ⁵⁶ Abraham, your ancestor, was very happy to see my day; he saw it and was glad."

⁵⁷ Then the Jewish leaders said to Jesus, "You are not yet 50 years old—and you have seen Abraham?"

⁵⁸ Jesus said to them, "I am telling you the truth: I was alive before Abraham was born!"

⁵⁹ They picked up stones to throw at Jesus, but he left the temple courtyard and kept out of sight.

A Man Born Blind

9 [1] As Jesus was walking along, he saw a man who had been born blind. [2] Jesus' followers asked him, "Rabbi, who sinned, this person or his parents, to cause him to be born blind?"

[3] Jesus answered, "This person did not sin; his parents did not sin. No, *this occurred*, so that God's deeds might be shown in this man's *life*.

[4] We must do the tasks of the One who sent me while it is still daytime. Night is coming. No one can work then. [5] I am light for the people of the world while I am in the world."

[6] After Jesus said these things, he spit on the ground and made some mud with it. Then he rubbed it on the blind man's eyes. [7] Jesus said to him, "Go, wash yourself in the pool of Siloam." (This word means "Sent.") Then the blind man went away and washed himself and came back with sight!

[8] Then the people who used to see him before (when he was a beggar) and his neighbors were saying, "This is the man who used to sit and beg!"

[9] Other people were saying, "It's him!" Still others were saying, "No, but he looks like him." But the man himself continued to say, "I'm the one!"

[10] They asked again and again, "How come you can see?"

[11] The man answered, "A man called Jesus made some mud and rubbed it on my eyes. Then he told me, 'Go to Siloam and wash yourself.' So I went there and washed myself, and now I can see!"

[12] They asked him, "Where is Jesus?" The blind man answered, "I don't know."

The Pharisees Question the Man

[13] They brought the man who was once blind to the Pharisees. [14] (Jesus had made the mud and opened the blind man's eyes on the Sabbath day.)

[15] Again, the Pharisees kept asking the blind man how he could see. The man said to them, "He put mud on my eyes, I washed myself, and I can see."

[16] Some of the Pharisees were saying, "This man is not from God because he does not keep the Sabbath day!" But others were asking, "How could a sinful man perform such miracles?" They were divided among themselves.

[17] They asked the man again, "What do you say about Jesus? *Do you believe* he opened your eyes?" The man answered, "He is a prophet."

[18] The Jewish leaders didn't believe that the man had really been blind and could now see, until they called the man's parents. [19] The leaders asked them, "Is this man your son? Do you claim that he was born blind? How come he now sees?"

[20] Then his parents answered, "We know he is our son and that he was born blind, [21] but we don't know how he can see now. We don't know how he opened his eyes. Ask him. He is a grown man; he can speak for himself." [22] (The man's parents said these things, because they were afraid of the Jewish leaders. The Jewish leaders had already agreed that if anyone said that Jesus was the Messiah, that person

would be thrown out of the synagogue. [23] That is why his parents said, "He is an adult; ask him.")

[24] Then, a second time, the Jewish leaders told the man (who had been blind), "Give glory to God! We know that this man is a sinner."

[25] The man answered, "Maybe he is a sinner. I don't know. But one thing I do know, I was blind and now I can see."

[26] They asked him, "What did he do to you? How did he open your eyes?"

[27] The man answered, "I have already told you and you didn't listen. Why do you want to hear it again? You don't want to become his followers, do you?"

[28] Then they insulted the man saying, "You are Jesus' follower. We are Moses' followers. [29] We **know** that God has spoken to Moses. But we don't know where this Jesus comes from."

[30] The man answered them, "That is amazing! You don't know where Jesus comes from, and yet he opened my eyes! [31] We know that God does not listen to sinners, but God will listen to anyone who respects Him and obeys His will. [32] Since time began, no one has ever heard of anyone opening the eyes of a man born blind. [33] If Jesus did not come from God, he could not do anything."

[34] They answered him, "You were totally born in sin; you cannot teach us!" And they threw him out.

Jesus Finds the Man

[35] Jesus heard that the Jewish leaders had thrown the man out. Jesus found him and asked him, "Do you believe in the Son of Man?"

³⁶ The man answered, "Sir, who is he, so that I may believe in him?"

³⁷ Jesus said to him, "You have seen him and he is speaking to you right now!"

³⁸ The man said, "Lord, I believe." And he worshiped Jesus.

³⁹ Jesus said, "I came into this world, so that there can be a Judgment *Day*, so that the people who cannot see may see and those who *think they* can see may become blind."

⁴⁰ Some Pharisees who were with Jesus heard this. They said to him, "You don't think **we** are blind, too, do you?"

⁴¹ Jesus said to them, "If you were blind, you would be innocent, but, you are now claiming you can see. So, your guilt remains."

Jesus Is the Good Shepherd

10¹ "I am telling you the truth: If a man does not get into the sheep pen through the gate, but climbs in by some other way, he is either a robber or a bandit. ² The one who comes through the gate is the shepherd of the sheep. ³ The man who guards the gate opens the gate for him. The sheep know the shepherd's voice. The shepherd calls the name of each one of his sheep and leads them out. ⁴ After he has brought all his own sheep out, he walks ahead of them and the sheep follow him because they know his voice. ⁵ They would never follow a stranger; they would run away from him. They would not recognize a stranger's voice." ⁶ Jesus used this example *about sheep*, but the people didn't understand what he was talking about.

Abundant Life

[7] Therefore, Jesus spoke again, "I am telling you the truth: I am the gate for the sheep. [8] All those who came before me were either robbers or bandits, but the sheep didn't listen to them. [9] I am the gate. If anyone will go through me, he will be saved. He may come and go *as he pleases* and find plenty to eat. [10] Why does the robber come? Only to steal, kill, and destroy. I came, so that they might have life—to the fullest!

[11] "I am the good shepherd. The good shepherd gives his own life for the sheep. [12] A man who has been hired is not really a shepherd. The sheep do not belong to him. When he sees a wolf coming, he leaves the sheep and runs away. The wolf catches them and scatters them. [13] The man doesn't care about the sheep, because he is a hired man. [14] I am the good shepherd. I know my *followers*, and my *followers* know me, [15] just as my Father knows me and I know my Father. I will give my life for the sheep. [16] But I have some other sheep that are not in this flock. I must lead them, too. They will listen to my voice. Then they will be one flock and one shepherd. [17] *Do you know* why my Father loves me? Because, I will give my life, so that I may take it back. [18] No one takes it away from me. I am giving it of my own free will. I have the authority to give it and I have the authority to take it back. I received this order from my Father."

[19] Again, the Jewish people were divided because of these words.

[20] Many of them were saying, "He is crazy! He's insane! Why are you listening to him?"

[21] Others were saying, "These words don't *sound like* the words *of a crazy person.* Could a crazy man open the eyes of a blind man?"

They Hate Jesus

[22] It was winter. The time came for the Feast of Dedication in Jerusalem.

[23] Jesus was walking in the temple courtyard next to Solomon's Porch. [24] Some Jews gathered around him. They kept asking him, "How much longer will you make us wait? If you are the Messiah, tell us clearly!"

[25] Jesus answered them, "I told you, but you didn't believe. I am doing miracles with my Father's authority. These are telling the truth about me, [26] but you don't believe, because you are not my sheep. [27] My sheep listen to my voice. I know them. They follow me. [28] I give them eternal life. They will **never** be lost. No one will snatch them out of my hand.

[29] My Father is stronger than anyone. No one can snatch them from my Father's hand. He has given me all things. [30] My Father and I are united."

[31] Again, some Jews picked up stones to throw at Jesus and kill him.

[32] Jesus answered them, "I have shown you many good works from my Father. For which good work are you stoning me?"

[33] They answered him, "We are going to throw rocks at

you, not for any good work, but because you said some evil things against God! You are only a man, yet you are making yourself God."

[34] Jesus answered them, "This is written in your law: 'I said that you are gods

Psalm 82:6

[35] The message of God came to them, and since he said 'gods'—and the Scripture cannot be broken— [36] why are you claiming I am saying evil things against God when I said, 'I am God's Son'? The Father selected me and sent me into the world. [37] If I am not performing miracles from my Father, don't believe in me. [38] But, if I **am** doing them, even though you may not believe in me, believe in *the evidence* of the miracles. You must know, once and for all, that the Father is in me and I am in the Father."

[39] Once again, they were trying to arrest Jesus, but he slipped through their hands.

[40] Jesus went back across the Jordan River to the place where John was first immersing people. Jesus stayed there. [41] Many people came to him. They said, "John did not perform any miracles, but everything he said about Jesus is true." [42] Many people there believed in Jesus.

Lazarus Dies

11 [1] A man named Lazarus was sick. He and his sisters, Mary and Martha, were from the village of Bethany. [2] (Mary was the one who rubbed the Lord *Jesus'* feet with perfume and dried them with her hair.) Lazarus, the brother, was very sick. [3] The *two* sisters sent *a message* saying, "Listen, your friend, *Lazarus*, is very sick!"

⁴ When Jesus heard this, he said, "This sickness will not end in death. Instead, it will be for God's glory. This will be used to give glory to the Son of God."

⁵ Jesus loved Mary, Martha, and Lazarus. ⁶ When Jesus heard that Lazarus was sick, he stayed where he was for two days. ⁷ After that, Jesus said to his followers, "Let us go back to the land of Judea."

⁸ Jesus' followers said to him, "But Rabbi, the Jewish leaders are now trying to stone you to death! Do you want to go there again?"

⁹ Jesus answered, "There are twelve hours in a day. Someone who is walking in the daytime does not stumble; he sees the light in this world.

¹⁰ But a person may stumble when he walks at night because he has no light."

¹¹ After Jesus said these things, he told them this: "Our friend Lazarus is asleep, but I will go wake him up."

¹² Then Jesus' followers said to him, "Lord, he will be all right if he's asleep."

¹³ (Jesus was talking about the death of Lazarus. They thought Jesus was talking about natural sleep.)

¹⁴ Then Jesus told them plainly, "Lazarus has died! ¹⁵ For your sakes, I'm glad I was not there *when he died*. I want you to believe. Let us go to him."

¹⁶ Thomas (called The Twin) said to the other followers, "Let us go, too, so we can die with him!"

Jesus Comes

¹⁷ When Jesus came, he found that Lazarus had been put in the grave four days before. ¹⁸ The village of Bethany

was near Jerusalem, less than two miles away. [19] Many Jews had come to Martha and Mary to comfort them over their brother's death. [20] When Martha heard that Jesus was coming, she went to meet him, but Mary continued to sit in the house.

[21] Martha said to Jesus, "Lord, my brother would never have died, if you had been here. [22] But, even now, I know if you ask God, He would give you anything."

[23] Jesus said to her, "Your brother will rise from death."

[24] Martha said to Jesus, "I know that Lazarus will rise from death, when all people are raised on the last Day."

[25] Jesus answered her, "I am the resurrection and the life. The person who commits himself to me will live, even though he may die. [26] Every person who lives and commits himself to me will **never** die! Do you believe this?"

[27] Martha said to him, "Yes, Lord. I still believe that **you** are the Messiah, the Son of God, who comes into the world."

Jesus Calls for Mary

[28] After Martha said these things, she went back and secretly called Mary, her sister, telling her, "The Teacher is here; he is calling for you."

[29] When Mary heard this, she got up quickly and went to Jesus. [30] Jesus had not yet come into the village. He was still at the place where Martha had met him. [31] Some Jews were with Mary in the house, comforting her. When they saw Mary stand up quickly and leave, they followed her. They thought she was going to Lazarus' grave, to cry *some more* there.

³² When Mary came to where Jesus was and saw him, she fell down at Jesus' feet. She said, "Lord, if you had been here, my brother would not have died!"

³³ Jesus saw her crying and the Jews who had come with her crying, too. He felt very sorry and upset. ³⁴ Jesus said, "Where have you put Lazarus?" They said to him, "Lord, come and see." ³⁵ Tears came to his eyes.

³⁶ Then the Jews said, "Look how Jesus loved Lazarus!"

³⁷ But some of them said, "This man was able to open the blind man's eyes. Couldn't he have kept Lazarus alive?"

Jesus Brings Lazarus Back to Life

³⁸ When Jesus came to the grave, again he was deeply moved in his heart. It was a cave with a large stone placed in front of it. ³⁹ Jesus said, "Take the stone away!" Martha, the dead man's sister, said to him, "Lord, this is the fourth day; there is already a bad smell!"

⁴⁰ Jesus said to her, "I told you that if you would believe, you would see the glory of God." ⁴¹ Then they took the stone away. Jesus looked up to heaven and said, "Father, I am thankful that you are listening to me.

⁴² I know that you always listen to me, but I said this because of the crowd which is standing here. I want them to believe that You sent me."

⁴³ After Jesus said this, he cried out with a loud voice, "Lazarus! Come out!" ⁴⁴ The dead man came out. Lazarus' hands and feet were bound with pieces of cloth. His face was wrapped with a handkerchief. Jesus said to them, "Untie him and let him go."

⁴⁵ Many Jews had come to visit Mary. They saw the things which Jesus did. They believed in him. ⁴⁶ But some of them went off to the Pharisees and told them what Jesus had done. ⁴⁷ The most important priests and the Pharisees called a meeting. They asked each other, "What are we going to do? This man is performing many miracles! ⁴⁸ If we let him go on like this, everyone will believe in him. Then the Romans will come and take us away—our *holy* place and our nation." ⁴⁹ One of them was Caiaphas. He was the high priest that year. He said to them, "You know nothing! ⁵⁰ Don't you think it would be better for one man to die for the people, than for the whole nation to be destroyed?" ⁵¹ (Caiaphas did not say this on his own. But, since he was the high priest that year, he prophesied that Jesus was about to die for the Jewish nation. ⁵² And not only for them, but also so that *all* God's scattered children might be gathered together into one people.) ⁵³ From that day forward, they plotted to kill Jesus.

⁵⁴ So, Jesus was not moving around among the Jews openly anymore. Jesus left there for an area which was near the desert. It was a town called Ephraim. Jesus stayed there with his followers for a while.

⁵⁵ The time for the Jewish Passover Festival was near. Many people went from the country up to Jerusalem before the Passover began. They wanted to make themselves pure. ⁵⁶ These people were standing in the temple courtyard looking for Jesus. They were asking one another, "What do you think? Will Jesus come to the festival or not?" ⁵⁷ The most important priests and Pharisees had given an

order: "If anyone knows where Jesus is, he must tell us, so that we may arrest him."

Mary Prepares Jesus for Burial

12 [1] Six days before the Passover Festival, Jesus came to the town of Bethany. Lazarus was there—the one whom Jesus had raised from death. [2] They gave a dinner for Jesus. Martha was helping and Lazarus was one of the guests with Jesus. [3] Mary brought in about a pint of a very expensive perfume—pure nard. She rubbed it on Jesus' feet. Then she dried his feet with her hair. The house was filled with the smell of perfume.

[4] One of Jesus' followers was ready to turn against Jesus. This was Judas Iscariot. He said, [5] "Why wasn't this perfume sold for 300 silver coins and given to some poor people?" [6] (Judas did not say this because he cared about poor people. Judas was a thief; he was the one who was always carrying the *group's* bag of money.)

[7] Then Jesus said, "Leave her alone. She must do this for the day when I am buried. [8] You will always have the poor with you, but you will not always have **me**!"

People Come to See Lazarus

[9] A large crowd of Jews knew that Jesus was there. They came not only because they wanted to see Jesus, but also because of Lazarus, who had been raised from death. [10] The most important priests planned to kill Lazarus, too. [11] Many people were going away from the Jewish leaders because of Lazarus. They were beginning to believe in Jesus.

Jesus Enters Jerusalem

[12] The next day, a large crowd came to the festival. When they heard that Jesus was coming to Jerusalem, [13] they took branches from palm trees and went out to meet him. They were shouting, "Hosanna! Give praise to the king of Israel who is coming with the authority of the Lord *God*."

[14] Jesus found a young donkey and rode on it, as it is written:

[15] "Don't be afraid, city of Jerusalem. Look, your King is coming, sitting on a young donkey."

Zechariah 9:9

[16] At first, Jesus' followers didn't understand these things, but later, when Jesus was *raised to life* in glory, they remembered that these for him.

[17] There was a crowd with Jesus. They were always telling people about how Jesus called Lazarus from the grave, how he raised him from death. [18] This is why a crowd met Jesus. They heard that Jesus had performed this miracle. [19] Then the Pharisees said to one another, "Look! Nothing we do does any good. Everyone is following Jesus!"

Jesus Must Die So We May Live

[20] Some non-Jewish people had come up *to Jerusalem* to worship *God* at the festival. [21] They came to Philip, who was from the town of Bethsaida in Galilee. They kept saying to him, "Sir, we want to meet Jesus."

[22] Philip went and told Andrew. Andrew and Philip came and spoke to Jesus. [23] Jesus answered them, "The time has come for me to receive glory. [24] I am telling you the truth:

If one grain of wheat does not fall into the ground and die, it will always be just one grain of wheat, but if the grain dies, it will produce a large cluster. [25] The person who loves his own life is destroying it, but the person who does not value his life in this world will keep his life forever. [26] If anyone serves me, he must follow me. My servant will be where I am. If anyone serves me, the Father will honor that person."

Jesus Prays to His Father

[27] "My soul is very troubled now. What should I say: 'Father, save me from this time *of suffering*'? No, the reason I came was for this time.

[28] Father, bring glory to Your name!" Then a Voice spoke from heaven, saying, "I have brought glory to it and I will bring glory to it again."

[29] There was a crowd standing there. They heard the Voice, too. Some of them were saying, "It thundered!" Others were saying, "An angel has spoken to him!"

[30] Jesus answered, "This Voice did not speak for my sake—but for your sake. [31] The time has come for this world to be judged. The time has come for the ruler of this world to be thrown out. [32] When I am lifted high above the earth, I will attract everyone to me." [33] (Jesus was saying this to show what kind of death he was about to suffer.)

[34] The crowd answered him, "In the law, we have heard that the Messiah will live forever. How can you say that the Son of Man must be nailed to a cross? Who is this 'Son of Man'?"

³⁵ Jesus said to them, "The light is with you only for a little while longer. Travel while you have the light, so that darkness will not catch you. A person who is walking around in the dark doesn't know where he is going. ³⁶ Believe in the light while you have the light. You must be sons of light."

Many People Believe, but They Are Afraid

When Jesus had finished speaking, he went away and kept out of sight. ³⁷ People did not believe in Jesus, even though such proofs from God were in front of them. ³⁸ The message of Isaiah the prophet has come true: "Lord, who believed our report? To whom did the Lord God show His power?"

Isaiah 53:1

³⁹ They could not believe for the reason given by Isaiah: ⁴⁰ "Their eyes are blind because of God. Their hearts are hard because of God. Otherwise, they could see with their eyes and understand with their hearts and turn. Then I could heal them."

Isaiah 6:10

⁴¹ Isaiah said these things, because he saw Jesus' glory. Isaiah was talking about Jesus.

⁴² Many people, even some of the leaders, believed in Jesus. But they would not say that they believed, because they were afraid of the Pharisees. They didn't want to be thrown out of the synagogues. ⁴³ They loved praise from man more than praise from God.

Believing Jesus = Believing God, the Father

⁴⁴ Jesus cried out, "The person who believes in me is not only believing in **me**, but also in the One who sent me.

[45] The person who sees **me** sees the One who sent me.

[46] I have come like light into the world, so that every person who believes in **me** will not stay in the darkness. [47] If someone hears my words and does not obey them, I am not the one who judges him *now*. I came to save the world, not to judge it. [48] The person who rejects **me** and does not accept my words has something to condemn him—the very message which I spoke. That message will condemn him on the last day.

[49] I have not spoken on my own. The Father Himself sent me. He told me what to say. [50] I know that His command is eternal life. I am saying exactly what the Father said to me."

Jesus Washes Their Feet

13 [1] Just before the Passover Festival, Jesus knew that his time had come; He must pass from this world to the Father. Jesus loved his own people in the world; he loved them to the very end.

[2] It was time for the evening meal. The Devil had already put it in Judas' heart to turn against Jesus. (Judas Iscariot was the son of Simon.)

[3] Jesus knew that the Father had put everything into his hands. He knew that he had come from God and that he was going back to God. [4] Jesus got up from the evening meal and laid his clothes aside. He took a towel and wrapped it around his waist. [5] Then Jesus put water into a pan. He began to wash his followers' feet. He dried their feet with the towel which was around his waist. [6] Then Jesus came

to Simon Peter. Peter asked him, "Lord, are **you** going to wash my feet?"
⁷ Jesus answered him, "You may not understand what I am doing now, but you will understand it later."
⁸ Peter said to him, "You will **never** wash my feet!" Jesus answered him, "If I don't wash you, you are not sharing with me."
⁹ Simon Peter said to Jesus, "Lord, wash not only my feet; wash my hands and head, too!"
¹⁰ Jesus said to him, "The person who has already had a bath needs only to wash his feet *when they get dirty*; his whole body is clean. You are clean—but not all of you!"
¹¹ Jesus knew who was turning against him. That is why Jesus said, "Not all of you are clean!"
¹² After Jesus had washed their feet, he put on his clothes and sat down at the table again. He asked them, "Do you know what I have just done to you? ¹³ You call me 'Teacher' and 'Lord.' You are right, because I **am** the Teacher and the Lord. ¹⁴ Since I, the Lord and Teacher, washed your feet, you ought to wash one another's feet. ¹⁵ I have given you an example. You should do things *for others* as I have done for you. ¹⁶ I am telling you the truth: A slave is not more important than his master. A messenger is not more important than the one who sent him. ¹⁷ Since you know these things, you will be happy if you practice them. ¹⁸ I am not talking about all of you. I know the ones whom I have chosen. The Scripture must come true: 'The person who was eating my food turned against me.'

Psalm 41:9

¹⁹ I am telling you now, before it happens, so that when it does happen, you may believe that I am *the Messiah*. ²⁰ I am telling you the truth: If anyone accepts someone whom I send, he is accepting **me**, too! The person who accepts me is accepting the One who sent me." ²¹ After Jesus said these things, he was very troubled in his spirit. He told them openly, "I am telling you the truth: One of you will turn against me!"

"Do It Quickly!"

²² Jesus' followers began looking at one another. They were wondering which one he was talking about. ²³ One of his followers, (the one whom Jesus loved) was sitting very close to Jesus. ²⁴ Simon Peter signaled to this follower. Peter wanted him to ask Jesus, "Which one are you talking about?" ²⁵ So, that follower moved very close to Jesus and whispered to him, "Lord, who is it?"

²⁶ Jesus answered, "After I dip this piece of bread in the sauce, I will give it to that person." Then Jesus dipped a piece of bread into the sauce and gave it to Judas Iscariot, the son of Simon. ²⁷ When this happened, Satan went into Judas. Then Jesus said to him, "Do what you plan to do quickly!" ²⁸ None of the guests knew why Jesus said this to him. ²⁹ Since Judas kept the *group's* bag of money, some were thinking that Jesus meant: "Buy what we need for the feast." or "Give something to the poor people." ³⁰ So, Judas took the piece of bread and went out immediately. And it was night.

Love One Another

[31] After Judas left, Jesus said, "Now I am given glory and, in me, God is given glory. [32] Since God is given glory in me, God will give me glory for myself; He will do it immediately. [33] Little children, I am still with you a little while longer. Just as I said to the Jewish leaders, 'You will look for me, but where I am going you cannot come.' I am saying the same thing to you now. [34] I am giving you a new command—love one another. You must love one another, just as I loved you. [35] You must have love for one another. This is how everyone will know that you are **my** followers."

Would You Give Up Your Life for Me?

[36] Simon Peter said to Jesus, "Lord, where are you going?" Jesus answered him, "I am going where you cannot follow now, but you will follow later."

[37] Peter said to him, "Lord, why can't I follow you now? I would give up my life for you!"

[38] Jesus answered, "Would you give up your life for me? I am telling you the truth: Before the rooster crows *tomorrow morning,* you will say that you don't even know me. You will do it three different times!"

Don't Be Troubled

14 [1] "Don't let your heart be troubled. You trust in God; trust in me, too. [2] There are many rooms in my Father's house. I would have told you, if that were not true. I am taking a trip to prepare a place for you. [3] Since I am leaving to prepare a place for you, *you can be sure that I*

will come back and take you with me, so that you will be where I am. [4] You know the road to where I am going."

[5] Thomas said to Jesus, "Lord, we do not know where you are going. How can we know the way?"

[6] Jesus said to him, "**I am the way and the truth and the life!** The only way anyone can come to the Father is through **me**! [7] If you had known me, you would have known my Father. But even now, you do know Him and you have seen Him."

[8] Philip said to Jesus, "Lord, show us the Father; that would be enough for us."

[9] Jesus asked him, "Philip, have I been with you such a long time and you have not known me? The person who has seen **me** has seen the Father! How can you say, 'Show us the Father'? [10] You believe that I am in the Father and the Father is in me, don't you? The words which I am using to speak to you are not words I use on my own. The Father performs His miracles; He stays in me. [11] Believe me, I am in the Father and the Father is in me. At least believe, because of these miracles. [12] I am telling you the truth: The person who believes in me will do the same deeds that I am performing. He will do even greater things than these. I am going to the Father. [13] I will do whatever you ask for in my name. The Father will receive glory in the Son. [14] If you ask me for something in my name, I will do it."

The Holy Spirit

[15] "If you love me, obey my commands. [16-17] I will ask my Father and He will give you another Comforter—the

Spirit of truth. He will be with you forever. The people of the world cannot accept him, because they don't see him or know him, but you know him because he stays with you—he is in you ¹⁸ I will not abandon you, as though you were orphans. I am coming to you. ¹⁹ A little longer and the people of the world will not see me anymore. However, **you** will see me. You will live, because I live. ²⁰ At that time, you will know that I am in my Father, you are in me, and I am in you. ²¹ The person who accepts my commands and obeys them is the one who truly loves me. My Father will love the person who loves me, and I will love him and make myself known to him."

²² Judas (not Judas Iscariot) said to Jesus, "Lord, what has happened that you are ready to reveal yourself to **us**, but not to the people of the world?"

²³ Jesus answered him, "If anyone loves me and obeys my teaching, my Father will love him. We will come and live with him. ²⁴ The person who does not love me will not obey my teachings. The message you are hearing is not mine; it belongs to the Father who sent me.

²⁵ "I have said these things to you while I am staying with you. ²⁶ The Comforter will teach you everything. He will cause you to remember everything I have told you. He is the Holy Spirit. The Father will send him with my authority. ²⁷ I am leaving peace with you. I am giving you my peace. This peace that I am giving you is not like *the type that* the world gives. Don't let your heart be troubled or afraid.

²⁸ "You have heard me say: 'I am leaving, but I will come back to you.' If you really loved me, you would be glad that

I am traveling to the Father. The Father is greater than I am. [29] Now I have told you before it happens, so that when it happens, you will believe. [30] I will not say many more things while I am with you. The ruler of the world is coming. He can do nothing to me. [31] I must do as my Father ordered me, so that the people of the world may know that I love the Father. Get up! Let us go away from here."

Jesus Is the True Vine

15 [1] "I am the true vine. My Father is the farmer. [2] My Father takes away any branch in me which is not producing fruit. My Father trims each branch which is producing fruit, so that it will produce more fruit. [3] You are already clean, because of the message I have spoken to you. [4] Stay in me and I will stay in you. No branch can produce fruit on its own; it must stay on the vine. In the same way, you cannot *produce*, unless you stay in **me**. [5] I am the vine; you are the branches. Who will produce much fruit? The person who stays in me and in whom I stay. You can do nothing without me! [6] If someone does not stay in me, he is like a branch which is thrown away. He dries up. People gather *dead* branches and throw them into the fire, and they burn up. [7] If you stay in me and my words stay in you, then you may ask for whatever you want and it will happen for you. [8] You must produce much fruit and be my followers. This is how my Father gets glory. [9] I love you, just as the Father loves me. Stay in my love. [10] I have obeyed my Father's commands and I stay in His love. If you obey my commands, you will stay in my love.

¹¹ "I have said these things to you, so that my joy may be in you and your joy may be complete. ¹² This is my command: Love one another, as I have loved you. ¹³ Suppose someone gives up his life for his friends. No one has a greater love than this.

¹⁴ "You are my friends, if you do what I tell you to do. ¹⁵ I am no longer calling you 'slaves,' because a slave doesn't know what his master is doing. I am calling you 'friends,' because I have revealed to you everything which I have heard from my Father. ¹⁶ You did not choose me; I chose you! I have appointed you to go and produce fruit. Your fruit will last. My Father will give you whatever you ask for in my name. ¹⁷ Love one another! I am ordering you to do this."

THE COMFORTER WILL TEACH YOU
EVERYTHING. HE WILL CAUSE YOU TO
REMEMBER EVERYTHING I HAVE TOLD YOU
(JOHN 14:26).

The World will Hate You, Too!

¹⁸ "If the people of the world hate you, remember that they hated **me** first. ¹⁹ If you were from the world, the people of the world would love their own people. I chose you from

out of the world. You are not in the world *anymore*. That is why the people of the world hate you. [20] Do you remember the lesson I taught you: 'No slave is more important than his master'? Since they persecuted me, they will persecute you. Since they obeyed my teaching, they will obey your teaching. [21] The people of the world will do all these things to you, because of my name; they didn't know the One who sent me. [22] If I had not come and talked to them, they would not be so guilty, but now, they have no excuse for their sin. [23] A person who hates **me** hates my Father, too. [24] They would not be so guilty if I had not performed deeds among them which no one has ever done. But they have now seen *the miracles*. They have hated me and my Father. [25] *It was necessary* for this verse written in their law to come true: 'They have no reason to hate me.'

Psalm 35:19

[26] "I will send you the Comforter from the Father. He is the Spirit of truth who is coming out from the Father. When he comes, he will tell the truth about me. [27] You will testify, too, because you were with me from the very beginning."

They'll Throw You Out!

16[1] "I have said these things to you, so that you will not be led into sin. [2] They will throw you out of the synagogues. The time is coming when each person who kills you will think he is offering service to God. [3] They don't know the Father or me. That is why they will do these things. [4] But I have told you these things, so when the time comes, you will remember that I warned you. "I did not tell you this in the beginning because I was with you, ⁵ but now I am going to the One who sent me. Not one of you is asking me, 'Where are you going?' ⁶ You feel very sad, because I have told you these things. ⁷ But I am telling you the truth; if I leave, it is really better for you. If I don't leave, the Comforter won't come to you. However, if I go away, I will send him to you. ⁸ He will prove that the people of the world are wrong about sin, wrong about what is right, and wrong about judgment: ⁹ about sin, because they are not believing in me; ¹⁰ about what is right, because I am going to the Father and you will not see me anymore; ¹¹ about judgment, because the ruler of this world has been condemned.

¹² "I still have many things to tell you, but you cannot take it right now.

¹³ When the Spirit of truth comes, he will guide you into all truth. He will not speak on his own *authority*. He will say whatever he hears. He will tell you about things to come. ¹⁴ He will give me glory. He will take what I am saying and will tell it to you.

¹⁵ Everything that belongs to my Father belongs to me, too. This is why I said, 'He will take what I am saying and tell it to you.' "

In a Little While

¹⁶ *Jesus said,* "In a little while, you will not see me anymore, but then, after a little while, you will see me!" ¹⁷ Some of Jesus' followers said to one another, "What is the meaning of what he told us: 'In a little while, you will not see me

anymore, but then, after a little while, you will see me,' and 'I am going to the Father'? [18] What does this 'little while' mean? We don't know what he is talking about!" [19] Jesus knew that they were wanting to ask him a question. He said to them, "Were you arguing with one another about what I said: 'In a little while, you won't see me anymore, but then, after a little while you will see me'? [20] I am telling you the truth: You will cry and be sad, but the people of the world will be glad. You will be full of sorrow, but your sorrow will change into joy. [21] When a woman is giving birth, she has much pain. Her time has come. But, after the child is born, she no longer remembers the suffering; she is so happy that a human being is born into the world. [22] You may have pain now, but I will see you again. Your heart will be glad. No one will be able to take your joy away from you. [23] At that time, you will ask me no questions. I am telling you the truth: The Father will give you whatever you ask for in my name. [24] So far, you have not asked for anything in my name. Ask *now*, and you will receive. Your joy will be complete."

YOU DID NOT CHOOSE ME; I CHOSE YOU!
(JOHN 15:16)

Jesus Is Going Home

²⁵ "I have used symbolic examples to tell you about these things. The time is coming when I will no longer use examples like that. I will speak plainly to you. I will tell you about the Father. ²⁶ At that time, you will use my name to ask for things. I am not saying that I will ask the Father for your sake. ²⁷ The Father Himself loves you, because you have loved me and have believed that I came from God. ²⁸ I did come from the Father and I have come into the world. But now, I am leaving the world and going back to the Father."

²⁹ Jesus' followers said, "Listen, now you are talking plainly. You are not using figurative language anymore. ³⁰ Now we **know** that you know everything! There is no need for anyone to ask you more questions. This is why we believe that you came from God."

³¹ Jesus asked them, "Do you believe now? ³² Listen, the time is coming—it's already here—when you will all be scattered, every man for himself. You will abandon me. However, I am really not alone; the Father is with me. ³³ I have said these things to you, so that you may have peace in me. You will have trouble in the world, but be strong; I have conquered the world."

Jesus' Prayer

17 ¹ After Jesus said these things, he looked up to heaven and said, "Father, the time has come. Bring glory to Your Son, so that Your Son may bring glory to You. ² You have given him authority over all mankind.

To each one that You have given the Son, You will give eternal life. ³ This is eternal life: that they may know You, the only true God, and Jesus Christ, the one whom You sent. ⁴ I have brought You glory on the earth. I finished the work which You gave me to do. ⁵ Now, Father, give me glory—the glory I had with You when I was with You before the world existed.

⁶ "I have revealed Your name to men. You gave these men to me from the world. They were Your people and You gave them to me. They have obeyed Your teaching. ⁷ They now know that everything You have given me comes from You. ⁸ I have given them the words which You gave me. They have received them. They knew I really did come from You. They believed that You sent me.

YOU WILL HAVE TROUBLE IN THE WORLD, BUT BE STRONG; I HAVE CONQUERED THE WORLD (JOHN 16:33).

---

⁹ "I am praying for them, not for the world. I am praying for those men You have given me, because they belong to You. ¹⁰ Everything that is mine is Yours. Everything that is Yours is mine, too. In them I have received glory. ¹¹ I am not in

the world anymore, but my apostles are in the world. I am coming to You. Holy Father, keep them in Your name, the name which You have given me. May they be united, as we are. [12] When I was with them, I was always keeping them in Your name, the name You have given me. I have protected them. Not one of them was lost—only the child of destruction. The Scripture must come true. [13] Now I am coming to You. I am saying these things in the world, so that these men may have my complete joy in them. [14] I have given them Your message. The people of the world hated them, because they don't come from this world. I am not from this world, either. [15] I do not pray that You take them out of the world—just keep them from the evil one. [16] I don't come from the world; they don't come from the world, either. [17] Your message is the truth. May the truth make them holy! [18] I sent them into the world, just as You sent me into the world.

[19] "I keep myself holy for them, so that they will be holy by the truth.

[20] "I pray not only for my apostles, but also for the people who believe in me through their teaching. [21] May all of them be united, just as You are in me and I am in You. I pray that they will be in us, so that the people of the world may believe that You sent me. [22] I have given them the glory that You have given me. May they be united, as we are; [23] I in them and You in me. May they be completely united, so that the people of the world will know that You sent me and that You loved them as You loved me.

²⁴ "Father, You loved me before the world was created. You have given me glory. I want them to see it. I want them to be with me, where I will be.

²⁵ "Righteous Father, the people of the world do not know You, but I know You. These men here know that You sent me. ²⁶ I revealed Your name to them and I will reveal it. I want them to have Your love in them, the same love that You have for me. I want to be in them, too."

Jesus Prays in the Garden

18¹ After Jesus had said these things, he and his followers went across Kidron Creek, where there was a garden. They went into the garden. ² Judas (the one who turned against Jesus) also knew the place. Jesus often met there with his followers. ³ Then Judas took a group of soldiers and some *temple* guards sent by the most important priests and Pharisees. They had torches, lanterns, and weapons. ⁴ Jesus knew everything which was going to happen to him. He stepped forward and said to them, "Who are you looking for?"

⁵ They answered him, "Jesus from Nazareth." Jesus said to them, "I am the one." Judas (the one who turned against Jesus) was standing there with them. ⁶ When Jesus said, "I am the one," they drew back and fell to the ground. ⁷ Jesus asked them again, "Who are you looking for?" They said, "Jesus from Nazareth."

⁸ Jesus answered, "I told you that I am the one. Since you are looking for **me**, let these men go free." ⁹ (Jesus said that to make this come true: "I have not lost one of those You have given me.")

[10] Simon Peter had a sword. He struck the high priest's servant, cutting off his right ear. (The servant's name was Malchus.) [11] Then Jesus said to Peter, "Put your sword back into its place! My Father has given me this cup *of suffering*. Shouldn't I drink it?"

They Arrest Jesus

[12] The commanding officer, his group of soldiers, and the Jewish *temple* guards arrested Jesus and tied him up. [13] They brought him first to Annas who was Caiaphas' father-in-law. Caiaphas was the high priest that year. [14] (He had advised the Jewish leaders that it would be better for one man to die for all of the people.)

Peter Falls Away

[15] Simon Peter and another follower went along behind Jesus, but the high priest knew the other follower. This man went with Jesus into the high priest's courtyard. [16] Peter stood outside at the gate. The other follower, the one known to the high priest, went outside and told the gatekeeper to let Peter come in. [17] The girl who was the gatekeeper said to Peter, "**You** are one of this man's followers, aren't you?" Peter answered, "I am not."

[18] The servants and the guards were standing there. They had made a fire, because it was cold. They were warming themselves. Peter stood with them and warmed himself, too.

[19] The high priest asked Jesus about his followers and about his doctrine.

²⁰ Jesus answered him, "I have spoken plainly to the world. I always taught where Jewish people gather—in *the* synagogues and in the temple courtyard. I have said nothing secretly. ²¹ Why ask me? Ask those who heard me. Look, they know what I said." ²² When Jesus said this, one of the guards who was standing there struck Jesus. This man asked, "Is that the way to answer the high priest?"

²³ Jesus answered him, "If I said something wrong, show me what it was. If it was good, then why did you hit me?"

²⁴ Then Annas sent Jesus down to Caiaphas.

²⁵ Simon Peter was still standing there warming himself. Then they said to him, "**You** are one of Jesus' followers, aren't you?" Peter said it was not true. He said, "I am not!"

²⁶ One of the high priest's servants said, "I saw you with Jesus in the garden." (This man was a relative of Malchus. Peter had cut off Malchus' ear.)

²⁷ Again, Peter denied it. Immediately the rooster crowed.

They Bring Jesus to Pilate

²⁸ Then they took Jesus from Caiaphas to the *Roman* fortress. It was early in the morning. They didn't go into the fortress. They didn't want to be made unclean, so that they could not eat the Passover lamb. ²⁹ So Pilate went outside where they were. He asked, "What charge are you making against this man?"

³⁰ They answered Pilate, "If he were not a criminal, we would not be giving him to you."

³¹ Pilate said to them, "**You** take him and judge him by your

own law." Then the Jewish leaders said to him, "*Under Roman law*, it is not legal for us to execute anyone." ³² (The Jewish leaders said this, so that what Jesus said would come true. This was showing what kind of death Jesus was about to suffer.)

³³ Pilate went back into the fortress. He called for Jesus and asked him, "Are **you** the King of the Jews?"

³⁴ Jesus answered, "Are you saying this on your own, or did someone else tell you this about me?"

³⁵ Pilate answered, "I am not a Jew, am I? The leading priests and your own people turned you over to me. What have you done?"

³⁶ Jesus answered, "My kingdom does not come from this world. If it did, my servants would be fighting to keep the Jewish leaders from giving me to you. My kingdom is not from here."

³⁷ Pilate said to him, "So then, you **are** a king!" Jesus answered, "You say that I am a king. The reason I was born, the reason why I have come into the world is to give evidence for the truth. Every person who listens to my voice comes from *the* truth."

³⁸ Pilate asked, "What **is** truth?" After this, Pilate went back out to the Jewish leaders. He said to them, "I find nothing to charge this man with. ³⁹ You have a custom that I set one *prisoner* free at each Passover time. You decide; should I set the King of the Jews free?"

⁴⁰ They yelled, "No! Not this man! Set Barabbas free." (Barabbas was a criminal.)

Jesus must Die on the Cross

19 [1] Then Pilate took Jesus and had *them* whip him.
[2] The soldiers made a crown out of thorny branches.
They put it on Jesus' head and put a purple robe on him.
[3] They kept coming up to Jesus and saying, "Hail! O King
of the Jews!" They hit him many times.

[4] Pilate went back out and spoke to them, "Look, I am
bringing him out to you, so that you will know that I find
nothing wrong with him."

[5] Then Jesus came out. He was wearing the thorny crown
and the purple robe. Pilate said to them, "Look at the
man!"

[6] When the most important priests and the *temple* guards
saw Jesus, they shouted, "Nail him to a cross! Nail him to
a cross!" Pilate said to them, "You take him and nail him
to a cross! I find nothing wrong with him."

[7] But the Jewish leaders answered him, "We have a law.
According to the law, he must die, because he made
himself God's Son!"

[8] When Pilate heard this statement, he was even more
afraid. [9] So Pilate went back into the fortress and asked
Jesus, "Where do you come from?" Jesus did not give him
an answer.

[10] Then Pilate said to him, "Aren't you speaking to me?
Surely you must know I have authority to set you free and
I have authority to nail you to a cross!"

[11] Jesus answered Pilate, "You have no authority over me
at all, unless it has been given to you by God! That is why
the man who gave me to you has even more guilt."

[12] From this time on, Pilate tried hard to set Jesus free. But the Jewish leaders continued to yell, "If you set this man free, you are not Caesar's friend! Anyone who makes himself a king is against Caesar!"
[13] When Pilate heard these words, he brought Jesus outside. Pilate sat down on the judge's seat. He was at a place called The Stone Pavement. (In the Aramaic language the name was Gabbatha.) [14] It was about noon on the day before the Passover. Pilate said to the Jewish leaders, "Look, your King!"
[15] They yelled, "Take him away! Take him away! Nail him to a cross!" Pilate said to them, "Should I nail your King to a cross?" The most important priests answered, "The only King we have is Caesar!" [16] Then Pilate turned Jesus over to them to be nailed to the cross. So they took hold of Jesus.

Jesus on the Cross

[17] Jesus was carrying his own cross. He went out to a place which was called Skull Place. (In Aramaic it is Golgotha.)
[18] This is where they nailed him to the cross, along with two other men. Jesus' cross was between the crosses of the other two men.
[19] Pilate made a sign and put it on Jesus' cross. It read: JESUS FROM NAZARETH, THE KING OF THE JEWS
[20] Many Jewish people read this sign. This place was near the city of *Jerusalem*. The sign was written in Aramaic, Latin, and Greek. [21] The most important Jewish priests

kept saying to Pilate, "Don't write, 'The King of the Jews'! Instead, you should write, 'This man **said**, "I am the King of the Jews." ' "

²² Pilate answered, "What I have written stays written!"

²³ After the soldiers had nailed Jesus to the cross, they took his clothes and divided them into four parts—one for each soldier but the robe *remained*. This robe was seamless—completely made of one piece of woven cloth. ²⁴ They said to one another, "Let's not tear it. Let's gamble for it, to see who will get it!" *This happened* to make this Scripture come true: "They divided my clothes among them. They gambled for my clothing."

Psalm 22:18

That is what the soldiers did.

²⁵ Jesus' mother, his mother's sister, Mary the *wife* of Clopas, and Mary, from the town of Magdala, stood near the cross. ²⁶ Jesus saw his mother and the follower whom he loved standing there. He said to his mother, "Woman, look at your son." ²⁷ Then Jesus said to that follower, "Look at your mother." From that moment on, that follower accepted Mary as his own mother.

Jesus Dies!

²⁸ After this, when Jesus knew that everything was finished, he said this to make the Scripture come true: "I am thirsty." ²⁹ There was a jar full of sour wine nearby. So they soaked a sponge in it and put it on along stick. Then they brought this to Jesus' mouth. ³⁰ After Jesus drank some of it, he said, "It is finished!" Then he bowed his head and died.

³¹ The Jewish leaders did not want the bodies to stay on the crosses during the Sabbath day. This Sabbath was a very important one. So, since it was Friday, they asked Pilate to *hurry their death* by breaking their legs. Then they could carry them away. *Pilate allowed it.* ³² The soldiers came to the first man and broke his legs, and then to the other man who had been nailed to a cross, too. ³³ But when they came to Jesus, they saw that Jesus was already dead. They did not break his legs,
³⁴ but one of the soldiers did plunge his spear into Jesus' side. Immediately, blood and water flowed out. ³⁵ The person who saw it has given proof. His testimony is true. You know he is speaking the truth. **You** must believe, too. ³⁶ These things happened to make this Scripture come true: "Not one of his bones will be broken."

Exodus 12:46

³⁷ Another Scripture says, "They will look upon the one they wounded."

Zechariah 12:10

Joseph of Arimathea

³⁸ After this, Joseph, a man from the town of Arimathea, asked Pilate if he could take Jesus' body away. Joseph was a secret follower of Jesus, because he was afraid of the Jewish leaders. Pilate allowed Joseph to do this. Then Joseph came and took Jesus' body away. ³⁹ Nicodemus came, too. (Earlier he had come to Jesus at night.) He mixed myrrh and aloes together and brought about 75 pounds of it. ⁴⁰ The two men took Jesus' body and wrapped it in sheets

with the sweet-smelling spices. (This is the way Jews bury their dead.) ⁴¹ The place where Jesus was nailed to the cross was next to a garden. The garden had a new tomb in it. No one had been put there yet. ⁴² *There was not much time*—it was Friday. So, because the tomb was near, they placed Jesus in it.

The Empty Tomb

20 ¹ It was very early on Sunday morning. It was still dark. Mary (the one from Magdala) came to the tomb. She saw the stone moved away from the tomb.

² Then she ran and came to Simon Peter and the other follower whom Jesus loved. She said to them, "They have taken away the Lord *Jesus* from the tomb! We don't know where they put him!"

³ Then Peter and the other follower left. They went to the tomb. ⁴ Both of them were running, but the other follower outran Peter. He arrived at the tomb first. ⁵ He bent down and saw the sheets, but he did not go inside.

⁶ Then Simon Peter came, following. Peter went into the tomb. He also saw the sheets lying there. ⁷ But the handkerchief which had been on Jesus' face was not lying with the sheets. Instead, it was all alone, folded in one place. ⁸ Then the other follower, who had come to the tomb first, also went in. He saw and he believed. ⁹ (They did not yet know the Scripture which said that Jesus must rise from death.) ¹⁰ The two followers went back home.

Jesus Appears to Mary

¹¹ Mary was standing outside the tomb, crying while she was praying. She bent down and looked *into the tomb*.

¹² She saw two angels dressed in white. They were seated where Jesus' body had been lying—one at the head and one at the foot. ¹³ They asked her, "Woman, why are you crying?" She answered them, "They took my Lord away. I don't know where they put him."

¹⁴ After she said this, she turned around. She saw Jesus standing there, but she didn't know that it was Jesus.

¹⁵ Jesus said to her, "Woman, why are you crying? Who are you looking for?" Thinking that Jesus was the gardener, she said to him, "Mister, if you carried him off, tell me where you put him and I will take him away."

¹⁶ Jesus said to her, "Mary!" She turned and said to Jesus in Aramaic, "Rabboni!" (This word means "My Teacher!")

¹⁷ Jesus said to her, "Don't cling to me; I have not yet gone up to the Father. Go to your brothers and tell them this: 'I am going to my Father and your Father, to my God and to your God.' "

¹⁸ Mary (the one from Magdala) went and told the followers, "I have seen the Lord *Jesus*!" She told them that he had talked with her.

Jesus Appears Again

¹⁹ It was late that same Sunday. The doors were locked where the followers were gathered. They were afraid of the Jewish leaders. Jesus came and stood in the middle of them. He said to them, "Peace be to you."

²⁰ After Jesus said this, he showed them his hands and his side. When the followers saw the Lord *Jesus*, they were happy. ²¹ Then Jesus said to them again, "Peace to you. I am

sending you just as the Father has sent me." [22] After Jesus said this, he breathed on them and said, "Receive the Holy Spirit. [23] If you say some people are forgiven, then they are forgiven. But, if you say that the sins of some people are not forgiven, then they are not forgiven."

Doubting Thomas

[24] Thomas, (the one called The Twin) was one of the twelve *apostles*. He was not with them when Jesus came. [25] The other followers continued to tell him, "We have seen the Lord *Jesus!*" Thomas said to them, "I will never believe it, unless I see the marks of the nails in his hands, unless I put my finger into the marks of the nails, unless I put my hand into his side!"

[26] A week later, Jesus' followers were inside again. Thomas was with them, too. The doors were locked, but Jesus came and stood in the middle of them and said, "Peace to you." [27] Then Jesus said to Thomas, "Look at my hands! Put your finger here. Bring your hand here and put it in my side. Stop doubting, and start believing!"

[28] Thomas answered Jesus, "My Lord and my God!"

[29] Jesus said to him, "You have believed, because you have seen me. The happy ones are those who have not seen me and yet who believe."

Why This Book was Written

[30] Jesus showed many more proofs from God in front of his followers, but these are not written in this book. [31] These proofs have been written, so that you, the reader, might

believe this: Jesus is the Messiah, the Son of God. If you believe this, you will have *eternal* life by his name.

Jesus Appears in Galilee

21 [1] Later Jesus showed himself again to the followers at Lake Tiberias. This is the way he showed himself: [2] Simon Peter, Thomas (the one called The Twin), Nathanael (the one from the town of Cana in Galilee), the sons of Zebedee, and two more followers were all together. [3] Simon Peter said to them, "I am going fishing." They said to him, "We are coming with you." They went out and got into a boat. They caught nothing that night. [4] It was now early in the morning. Jesus stood on the shore, but the followers didn't know that it was Jesus. [5] Jesus said to them, "Young men, you haven't caught anything, have you?" They answered, "That's right."

[6] Jesus said to them, "Throw your net on the right side of the boat and you will find *some fish*." They did so. There were so many fish that they were no longer able to pull *the net into the boat*. [7] Then the follower whom Jesus loved said to Peter, "That is the Lord *Jesus!*" When Simon Peter heard this, he put on his clothes (he was stripped) and he jumped into the lake. [8] They were near the shore, about 100 yards away. The other followers came in the boat, dragging the net full of fish. [9] When they got to shore, they saw hot coals, with some fish and bread *cooking* on them. [10] Jesus said to them, "Bring some of the fish you just caught."

[11] Simon Peter got into the boat and dragged the net to shore. The net was full of big fish—153 of them! As large as they were, the net was still not torn.

¹² Jesus said to them, "Come, have breakfast!" None of the followers dared to ask Jesus, "Who are you?" They **knew** that he was the Lord.

¹³ Jesus went and got some bread and fish. He gave it to them. ¹⁴ This was now the third time that Jesus showed himself to the followers after he was raised from death.

Do You Love Me?

¹⁵ After they had eaten breakfast, Jesus asked Simon Peter, "Simon, *son of* John, do you love me more than these?" Peter answered him, "Yes, Lord, you know that I like you." Jesus said to him, "Feed my lambs."

¹⁶ Jesus asked Peter the second time, "Simon, *son of* John, do you love me?" Peter said to him, "Yes, Lord, you know that I like you." Jesus said to him, "Be a shepherd to my sheep."

¹⁷ Jesus asked him the third time, "Simon, *son of* John, do you like me?" Peter was sad, because the third time Jesus asked, "Do you **like** me?" Peter said to Jesus, "Lord, you know everything. You know that I like you!" Jesus said to him, "Feed my sheep. ¹⁸ I am telling you the truth, *Peter*, when you were young, you tied your own belt and you walked where you wanted to go. But when you get old, you will stretch out your hands and someone else will tie you. They will carry you where you don't want to go." ¹⁹ (Jesus said this to show what kind of death would be used to bring glory to God.) After Jesus said this, he said to Peter, "Follow me!"

Jesus Talks about John

[20] Peter turned and saw the follower coming behind them. (This was the man whom Jesus loved, the one who had been sitting at the table very close to Jesus who asked, "Lord, who is the one who is turning against you?") [21] When Peter saw this man, he said to Jesus, "Lord, and what about this man?"

[22] Jesus said to him, "If I want him to stay alive until I come, what business is it of yours? **You** follow me!" [23] So this rumor went out to the brothers: "That follower will not die." But Jesus did not say to him that he would not die. Jesus said, "If I want him to stay until I come, what business is it of yours?"

[24] He is the follower who wrote these things. He is the one who is giving proof about these things. We know that his testimony is true.

Conclusion

[25] There are many things which Jesus did. If each one of them were written down, I suppose that the whole world could not hold the books which could be written.

A Favor Please?

Please send me an e-mail at *publisher@destinyimage.com*. Let me know you have prayed and let me know you prayed this prayer. Tell me what's happening in your life. I will be sure to pray for you and have others pray for you, too.

God bless you!

Don Nori Sr.

ABOUT THE AUTHOR

Don Nori Sr. is the founder of Destiny Image Publishers and MercyPlace Ministries. MercyPlace Ministries is a non-profit renewal and revival ministry whose focus is to bring Jesus to a world that desperately needs Him.

www.mercyplace.com

In his current position as CEO of Destiny Image, Don spends most of his time writing and ministering internationally.

Visit Don Nori's Web site for itinerary, video blogs and new books

www.donnorisr.com

www.howtofindgodslove.org.

JOIN THE GOD'S LOVE MOVEMENT!

If this book has touched your life, please pass it on to someone else who needs to know His love.

We challenge you to partner with us to put this book in every home in America. Do you know 10 people who need to find God's Love? If so, accept the challenge and give a copy of this book to each person.

To find out more about this Movement, visit our Web site at: *www.howtofindgodslove.org.*

Or write to:

Destiny Image Publishers

P.O. Box 159

Shippensburg, PA 17257

Additional copies of this book and other
book titles from DESTINY IMAGE are
available at your local bookstore.

Call toll-free: 1-800-722-6774.

Send a request for a catalog to:

DDestiny
DImage®

Destiny Image® Publishers, Inc.

P.O. Box 310
Shippensburg, PA 17257-0310

*"Speaking to the Purposes of God for This
Generation and for the Generations to Come."*

**For a complete list of our titles,
visit us at www.destinyimage.com.**

www.ingramcontent.com/pod-product-compliance
Lightning Source LLC
Chambersburg PA
CBHW060756100426
42813CB00004B/838